THE GREEK TRAGEDY
IN NEW TRANSLATIONS

GENERAL EDITORS William Arrowsmith
and Herbert Golder

SOPHOCLES: Women of Trachis

THE GREEK TRAGEDY IN NEW TRANSLATIONS

General Editors: William Arrowsmith and Herbert Golder

Now available in paperback

AESCHYLUS

Persians
Translated by Janet Lembke and C. John Herington
Prometheus Bound
Translated by James Scully and C. John Herington
Seven Against Thebes
Translated by Anthony Hecht and Helen H. Bacon

EURIPIDES

Alcestis
Translated by William Arrowsmith
Hecuba
Translated by Janet Lembke and Kenneth J. Reckford

SOPHOCLES

Antigone
Translated by Richard Emil Braun
Oedipus the King
Translated by Stephen Berg and Diskin Clay
Women of Trachis
Translated by C.K. Williams and Gregory W. Dickerson

SOPHOCLES

Women of Trachis

Translated by
C. K. WILLIAMS

and
GREGORY W. DICKERSON

OXFORD UNIVERSITY PRESS
New York   Oxford

OXFORD UNIVERSITY PRESS

Oxford   New York   Toronto
Delhi   Bombay   Calcutta   Madras   Karachi
Petaling Jaya   Singapore   Hong Kong   Tokyo
Nairobi   Dar es Salaam   Cape Town
Melbourne   Auckland

and associated companies in
Berlin   Ibadan

First published in 1978 by Oxford University Press, Inc.,
200 Madison Avenue, New York, New York 10016
First issued as an Oxford University Press paperback, 1991

Oxford is a registered trademark of Oxford University Press

Library of Congress Cataloging in Publication Data
Sophocles.
Women of Trachis.
(The Greek tragedy in new translations)
Includes bibliographical references.
I. Williams, Charles Kenneth, 1936–
II. Dickerson, Gregory W., 1937–   III. Title.
PA4414.T7W5   882'.01   76-40740
ISBN 0-19-502050-2
ISBN 0-19-507009-7 (pbk.)

2 4 6 8 10 9 7 5 3

Printed in the United States of America

EDITOR'S FOREWORD

The Greek Tragedy in New Translations is based on the conviction that poets like Aeschylus, Sophocles, and Euripides can only be properly rendered by translators who are themselves poets. Scholars may, it is true, produce useful and perceptive versions. But our most urgent present need is for a re-creation of these plays—as though they had been written, freshly and greatly, by masters fully at home in the English of our own times. Unless the translator is a poet, his original is likely to reach us in crippled form: deprived of the power and pertinence it must have if it is to speak to us of what is permanent in the Greek. But poetry is not enough; the translator must obviously know what he is doing, or he is bound to do it badly. Clearly, few contemporary poets possess enough Greek to undertake the complex and formidable task of transplanting a Greek play without also "colonializing" it or stripping it of its deep cultural difference, its remoteness from us. And that means depriving the play of that critical otherness of Greek experience—a quality no less valuable to us than its closeness. Collaboration between scholar and poet is therefore the essential operating principle of the series. In fortunate cases scholar and poet co-exist; elsewhere we have teamed able poets and scholars in an effort to supply, through affinity and intimate collaboration, the necessary combination of skills.

An effort has been made to provide the general reader or student with first-rate critical introductions, clear expositions of translators' principles, commentary on difficult passages, ample stage directions, and glossaries of mythical and geographical terms encountered in the plays. Our purpose throughout has been to make the reading of the plays as vivid as possible. But our poets have constantly tried to remember that they were translating *plays*—plays meant to be produced, in language that actors could speak, naturally and with dignity. The poetry aims at being *dramatic* poetry and realizing itself in words and actions that are both speakable and playable.

Finally, the reader should perhaps be aware that no pains have been spared in order that the "minor" plays should be translated as carefully and brilliantly as the acknowledged masterpieces. For the Greek Tragedy in New Translations aims to be, in the fullest sense, *new*. If we need vigorous new poetic versions, we also need to see the plays with fresh eyes, to reassess the plays for *ourselves*, in terms of our own needs. This means translations that liberate us from the canons of an earlier age because the translators have recognized, and discovered, in often neglected works, the perceptions and wisdom that make these works ours and necessary to us.

A NOTE ON THE SERIES FORMAT

If only for the illusion of coherence, a series of thirty-three Greek plays requires a consistent format. Different translators, each with his individual voice, cannot possibly develop the sense of a single coherent style for each of the three tragedians; nor even the illusion that, despite the differences, the tragedians share a common set of conventions and a generic, or period, style. But they can at least share a common approach to orthography and a common vocabulary of conventions.

1. *Spelling of Greek Names*

Adherence to the old convention whereby Greek names were first Latinized before being housed in English is gradually disappearing. We are now clearly moving away from Latinization and toward precise transliteration. The break with tradition may be regrettable, but there is much to be said for hearing and seeing Greek names as though they were both Greek and new, instead of Roman or neo-classical importations. We cannot of course see them as wholly new. For better or worse certain names and myths are too deeply rooted in our literature and thought to be dislodged. To speak of "Helene" and "Hekabe" would be no less pedantic and absurd than to write "Aischylos" or "Platon" or "Thoukydides." There are of course borderline cases. "Jocasta" (as opposed to "Iokaste") is not a major mythical figure in her own right; her familiarity in her Latin form is a function of the fame of Sophocles' play as the tragedy *par excellence*. And as tourists we go to Delphi, not Delphoi.

The precisely transliterated form may be pedantically "right," but the pedantry goes against the grain of cultural habit and actual usage.

As a general rule, we have therefore adopted a "mixed" orthography according to the principles suggested above. When a name has been firmly housed in English (admittedly the question of domestication is often moot), the traditional spelling has been kept. Otherwise names have been transliterated. Throughout the series the -os termination of masculine names has been adopted, and Greek diphthongs (as in Iphigeneia) have normally been retained. We cannot expect complete agreement from readers (or from translators, for that matter) about borderline cases. But we want at least to make the operative principle clear: to walk a narrow line between orthographical extremes in the hope of keeping what should not, if possible, be lost; and refreshing, in however tenuous a way, the specific sound and name-boundedness of Greek experience.

2. Stage directions

The ancient manuscripts of the Greek plays do not supply stage directions (though the ancient commentators often provide information relevant to staging, delivery, "blocking," etc.) Hence stage directions must be inferred from words and situations and our knowledge of Greek theatrical conventions. At best this is a ticklish and uncertain procedure. But it is surely preferable that good stage directions should be provided by the translator than that the reader should be left to his own devices in visualizing action, gesture, and spectacle. Obviously the directions supplied should be both spare and defensible. Ancient tragedy was austere and "distanced" by means of masks, which means that the reader must not expect the detailed intimacy ("He shrugs and turns wearily away," "She speaks with deliberate slowness, as though to emphasize the point," etc.) which characterizes stage directions in modern naturalistic drama. Because Greek drama is highly rhetorical and stylized, the translator knows that his words must do the real work of inflection and nuance. Therefore every effort has been made to supply the visual and tonal sense required by a given scene and the reader's (or actor's) putative unfamiliarity with the ancient conventions.

3. Numbering of lines

For the convenience of the reader who may wish to check the English against the Greek text or vice versa, the lines have been numbered according to both the Greek text and the translation. The lines of the English translation have been numbered in mutiples of ten, and these numbers have been set in the right-hand margin. The (inclusive) Greek numeration will be found bracketed at the top of the page. The reader will doubtless note that in many plays the English lines outnumber the Greek, but he should not therefore conclude that the translator has been unduly prolix. In most cases the reason is simply that the translator has adopted the free-flowing norms of modern Anglo-American prosody, with its brief, breath- and emphasis-determined lines, and its habit of indicating cadence and caesuras by line length and setting rather than by conventional punctuation. Other translators have preferred four-beat or five-beat lines, and in these cases Greek and English numerations will tend to converge.

4. Notes and Glossary

In addition to the Introduction, each play has been supplemented by Notes (identified by the line numbers of the translation) and a Glossary. The Notes are meant to supply information which the translators deem important to the interpretation of a passage; they also afford the translator an opportunity to justify what he has done. The Glossary is intended to spare the reader the trouble of going elsewhere to look up mythical or geographical terms. The entries are not meant to be comprehensive; when a fuller explanation is needed, it will be found in the Notes

ABOUT THE TRANSLATION

This new translation of Sophocles' Women of Trachis is the work of one of America's most powerful and original poets and of a talented young Sophoclean scholar just beginning his career.

C. K. Williams is the forty-year-old author of three remarkable books of poetry. In 1969 he published his first book, Lies; this was followed in 1972 by I Am The Bitter Name. With Ignorance, his latest book, appeared in 1977 and was immediately greeted—deservedly—as a work of explosive and brilliant originality, one of the most important books of poetry to appear in the last two decades. Williams's collaborator, Professor Gregory Dickerson, holds a doctorate from Princeton where he wrote his dissertation on The Women of Trachis. At present he teaches Greek literature at Bryn Mawr College.

Like marriage, tandem translation is a tricky, even risky, business. Between poets and scholars there have often been walls, and sometimes wars. Both sides risk losing what, at times, seems to both to matter most. Creative compromise comes hard. It is anything but easy for a modern poet to grasp the complex demands, texture, and rhetoric in the dark language of a dead master whom he cannot reach except through the scholar's mediation. But it is often just as difficult for the scholar to mediate those matters which a poet, as opposed to a student or another scholar, must know in order to translate well; to distinguish, as he must, between what can be sacrificed and what cannot.

This version of *The Women of Trachis* proved, in the writing, no exception to the risks and trials of tandem translation. Success, like harmony, often eluded the collaborators. Indeed, there were months when I wondered whether the whole project might not dissolve in dispute. Progress was at times painfully slow; at one point communications almost broke down completely. Then, miraculously, word came that negotiations had been resumed; there was an intense bout of activity, and then weeks of fitfully excited, even exalted, progress and insight. Every line of the text was, it seemed to me, contested, and so, at times, was the central interpretation. But in disagreement they were sharpening their sense of the play's power, refining their differences by fighting them out, and then renewing the debate at a higher level.

In retrospect, what kept the collaboration alive was the passionate conviction, on both sides, that this play was, despite long centuries of neglect and disesteem, one of the greatest of Sophocles' plays, if not one of the most powerful of extant tragedies. If poet and classicist could not always bury or resolve their differences, they could make them creatively tense. For me at least, not a small part of the power of this version is this tense, edgy complexity; the absence from it of all bland or muffling compromise; a tough, because often embattled, variety; and, finally, a hard-won unity, as real as it is precarious, in which it is possible to feel both the turbulence of the original and the poet's final successful effort to bring that turbulence under firm artistic control.

It is not the business of the General Editor to take sides, or even to urge the virtues of the translators. But this play and this version are a special case. As for the play, I too am convinced that it is a staggering achievement, one of the very greatest of Greek plays. For sheer tragic power and horror, for sustained and concentrated vision, it is the equal of anything Sophocles wrote—superior in every way, I think, to *Electra* and even to *Antigone*. A great play, and an incredibly neglected one. Hence a special case. For one of the stated missions of the series is, by means of new poetic translations, to reclaim and if possible recover those plays unjustly scanted or dismissed by the conventional Victorian-Georgian "canon."

No play of Sophocles more deserves to be recovered. The brilliance and power are astonishing. I think, for instance, of the masterful symbolic account of eros in Herakles' "shirt of flame," the savage epiphany of love as an inward beast—an account surpassing even Euripides' more famous version in the *Medea*. Or of the intricately unified metaphors by which Sophocles expresses the idea of vicissitude and contingency in human life. Everywhere, in every way—in poetry, dance, theme, and structure—all expressive means are fused in the service of the elusive, paradoxical texture sought by the poet—the sense of life as fluid iridescence, a mercurial "shimmering" in which darkness is at first suffused with points of light, which then become light, which in turn blazes and burns before dissolving, like the centaur's robe, into darkness and dust. And we see, or rather feel, this texture danced out by the weaving feet of the chorus as a recurrent pattern, a pattern woven in the lives of men but also in the wheeling, the rising and falling of the constellations of the night sky, and the cresting and falling of the waves. Darkness and light in endlessly combined alternation; then the final revelation, when all the brightnesses converge, in the illumination of Zeus' lightning, like oracular truth revealed stabbing down on Oita where Herakles will ascend in flame.

Dramatic structure thus expresses the hero's career, itself a paradigm of human life at alternating intensities, both brutal and exalted. We see Herakles, consumed by the beast blazing inside him; at first overwhelmed, it seems, by pain and contingency, he then takes control of his life with a fierce, even radiant joy. We see him dying, yet forcing his son's hand with the purpose of outblazing—thereby defeating, destroying the beast blazing within. Dying, he asserts his own, as well as human, glory in a willed incandescence which no mere "accident" can diminish or darken. Herakles reveals himself as the son of Zeus, and this revelation of the son in turn reveals the father. God's lightning and hero's pyre fuse; human freedom is paradoxically resolved in compliance with the father's will. And the play closes with the pattern repeated as Herakles imposes on *his* son the obedience he shows to his own father, Zeus:

nothing,
none of all of it, that is not Zeus.

That we are required to see and feel these things strikes me as the outstanding virtue of this translation. It takes us where the play, if we are willing to follow, leads us. The language and the perception which inform it point to both mystery and illumination, in the confidence that both are actually *there*. We are not, as so often happens in translation, denied the profoundly contrary texture, the fused opposites, of tragedy; because the maze is truly made, the "way out" is also there. Revelation happens in a world made so terribly dark that it can be, as it should, blinding, even stunning.

One final point. The most original and, I think, far-reaching technical achievement of this version is the handling of the choral odes. Traditionally, the choruses of Greek tragedy are translated into the norms of what we know as the "personal lyric" for the simple reason that we have no convention that can accommodate poetry meant to be sung and danced collectively. Even the most striking efforts to translate Greek choral lyrics—I think of H.D.'s or perhaps of Ezra Pound's in his version of this play—are basically governed by the norms of the personal lyric of English tradition; which means that the dance, the song, the collective or generic power of the Greek are scanted or lost. Compare Williams's choruses with Pound's or H.D.'s, and one immediately sees the difference. What Williams renders is not simply the poetry, but the poetry as music, the poetry as dance—dance, music and poetry all fused in a fourth dimension of theatrical space and dramatic movement. Admittedly the version is not literal, but it is not "free" either in the sense that it ever abandons the Greek or invents itself, but only in the apposite intricacy of its reshaping and harmonic repetitions. The greatest single problem facing the translation of Greek tragedy is that of liberating drama from the tyranny of poetry (English lyric poetry, I mean, where the influence of Pound has been disastrous), and to recreate those forms—collective, musical, choreographic—without which Greek drama cannot be resuscitated as drama but only as poetry. If you happen to believe, as I do, that this is the central problem then the achievement of Williams and Dickerson here will seem an event of exceptional importance.

Baltimore, Maryland   WILLIAM ARROWSMITH

CONTENTS

Introduction, 3

Women of Trachis, 15

Translator's Comments, 73

Notes on the Text, 79

Glossary, 95

WOMEN OF TRACHIS

INTRODUCTION

Mutability; uncertainty; a universe of precipitous change: these are at the heart of three of the seven surviving tragedies of Sophocles. In *Ajax* the hero confronts abrupt changes in human values and relationships, recognizes them as part of the pattern of universal flux, and escapes submission by self-destruction. In *Oedipus* sight is annulled by blindness, illusion by truth, intellect by irrationality. But nowhere have these themes been elaborated with more urgency or austerity than in *Women of Trachis*. There are no gradual alterations in this tragedy, no subtle shifts of fortune, but stunning and total reversals, moving forward with the relentlessness of a turning wheel: thesis, crushing antithesis, and—at the moment of transformation—violence and destruction. This pattern of opposition and cyclicity prevails throughout the play. Things occur, occur again, in another form, to another person, until, by the end, characters, images, past and present, all seem to have fused under a single mask of human helplessness, of subjugation to time and change, of bitterness and defiance.

The *parodos*[1] serves as a programmatic statement of this design, prefiguring many of the tragedy's themes and movements. Cyclicity and opposition are embodied in its very architecture—in its return at the end to its initial image of "shimmering night" (132; 94)[2] and in its confinement of Herakles and Deianeira, the play's two principal op-

1. We have used this technical term for the entrance song of the Chorus as a matter of convenience. For the same reason we have used the traditional designations first stasimon, second stasimon etc. for the choral odes at 481ff, 616ff, 806ff, and 922ff. For both terms see the Glossary. The choral interlude at 201ff belongs to a separate category of brief, metrically asymmetrical songs.
2. All line numbers cited in the Introduction and Notes refer to the English translation.

3

posing figures, within isolated stanzas, just as they are isolated from each other in their lives and in the drama itself. Everything in the ode, in fact, is divided and at odds: night and day, darkness and light, sleep and consciousness, despair and hope, pain and exaltation.

The young women of the Chorus sing of life's mutability as a succession of alterations, of sudden comings and goings: "The shimmering night won't stay, wealth / won't, calamity won't, not / for humans won't at least, but suddenly, suddenly / it's disappeared, gone [aphar bebake], and someone else, some poor else, / is under them; the joy, the deprivation" (132-6). And the drama's past and present are punctuated by just such movements. Herakles arrives to confront Achelöos, and Deianeira is saved, only then herself to be "suddenly, gone [aphar bebakh']," torn from her mother (515f), and condemned to endless anxiety over the further comings and goings of her husband: "All I know is that he's disappeared [bebēken] again" (44). And later, when the truth—that the hero is now gone forever—comes home to Trachis, it comes with the same abruptness: ". . . look how suddenly, suddenly [aphar], it's come breaking / on us, the word, the godword . . ." (806f).

Like the constellations in their "spinning paths" (131) the themes of the parodos circle through the tragedy, as the shadow and light of pain and joy, loss and recovery, despair and hope play over the participants. The Messenger arrives to set the Chorus "spinning" (216) with the news that Herakles is finally coming home, but Deianeira's melancholy immediately returns, prompted by a characteristically Greek anxiety over the dangers implicit in her husband's success and then reinforced by her compassion for the victims of his triumph (286ff). Iole she pities most of all, for she sees mirrored in the young girl's fate her own subjection to peripety. Youth and beauty, which once, like some disembodied force, uprooted her from her virginal security, have whirled onward to strike at another (26; 41; 451). And this perception suddenly darkens the bright joy of Deianeira's initial response to the news of Herakles' return. (Cf. 196ff.) With the even more painful recognition of Herakles' faithlessness and destructive lust, Deianeira's gloom intensifies. She is driven to find hope in the darkness—the darkness of passion, in the love-charm which fuses the blood of Nessos, "the black-haired beast" (823), with the "black poison" of the Hydra (557f). But this hope too is taken from her, first fading into doubt over the propriety of her action and then obliterated by the dread inspired by the portent of the self-consuming wool. When Hyllos arrives to confirm her fear, she can only return to the despair in which she began the play. Joy, illusory, has come—and gone. Confronting the fulfillment of her premonition that her "deprivation" would be widowhood (172f), she chooses to die, leaving the Nurse to announce the violent irony that the wife, whose reunion with her husband was the focus of all her hope and energy, has, at the moment of his homecoming, "disappeared [bebēke] . . . her last journey" (855).

As the Chorus has predicted, it is now the turn of "someone else" to be stunned by peripety. The report which annihilates Deianeira's last hope begins by describing the new joy of Herakles and Hyllos— the son's happiness at seeing his father (738), and the hero's proud delight in the robe his wife has sent him. Then an ominous light begins to play over the account of the scene of sacrifice. The "bloody fires" start "blazing" (748); and within that image, flame against dark gore, shines the same lethal mutability possessed by the sun-slaughtered "shimmering night" of the parodos [aiola nuks: 94; 132], the "shimmering" serpentine metamorphosis of Achelöos [aiolos drakon: 14] and the "shimmering" Hydra [aiolos drakon: 818] whose venom strikes at Herakles from within Deianeira's gift of love. The pain which Herakles' own arrow struck long before into the "side" of the centaur Nessos (664) comes back to him, clinging to his "sides" (751) and ruthlessly devouring him. And onward the agony drives, to strike Deianeira, too, in "the side, where life lives" (904) and then Hyllos, lying "side by side" with her corpse, crying over his double loss (913ff).

Death brings Deianeira back to her marriage bed. In the final scene her husband's circle closes. Hyllos has rescued his father from the "shrouds of smoke" (779f) but not from the darkness from which it swirled. Herakles appears in a death-like sleep; he awakens to vindictive desperation (991f; 1067ff). Then the moment of his enlightenment arrives, the realization that the radiance of his mortal heroism has been smothered in the robe's embrace: "Finished! FINISHED! My light—it's over now" (1094). But there is one more light to be. The oracles which Herakles has received from his father, Zeus, become "clear" now, "brilliant" (1124), leading him to surrender to the light itself, to fire lit with a "flaming torch" (1148). To consummate this last heroic act he returns to the shelterless expanses from which he came, confident that there he will rediscover "joy" (1213).

II

It is this thematic flux which gives the tragedy its surface tension. But there is an even deeper theme, a particular aspect of mutability which Sophocles has selected from the myth and emphasized throughout the play. This is the constant resurgence of irrational bestiality in the world, the tragic, primeval struggle of civilized humanity to stifle or exclude the savagery and violence which threaten it both from without and from within.

Sophocles' obsession with this theme is vividly evident in his treatment of Deianeira. He has given her a rich psychological complexity which makes her one of the more memorable figures in Greek tragedy. But, more important, he has also shaped her to embody humanity's fundamental desire to achieve that secure stability which serves as the basis of civilized life; and in so doing, he has both drastically altered and refined the Deianeira tradition current at the time of the play's composition.

In that tradition, Deianeira entered the Herakles myth only after the end of his labors for Eurystheus; that is, she was merely the last of that restless hero's many women. Sophocles, by contrast, has raised her to the status of legitimate wife in a marriage which has lasted throughout Herakles' adult career. By so doing he has created a counterpoise to Herakles' world of challenge, change, and movement—a potential for the permanence of a securely rooted family. At the same time, he has carefully excluded all elements of Deianeira's traditional background which might clash with her function as a single-minded domesticating—and domesticated—force. No hint is given of the original Amazonian persona to which her name—"Fighter-with-men" or "Hostile-to-men," or even "Man-killer"—attests, a role in which she was long remembered, even after Sophocles' very different Deianeira had come to dominate the literary tradition, as a woman who "drove a chariot and practiced the arts of war."[3] In fact, with the exception of a few references to her father Oineus, the poet has obliterated all traces of her fierce Aitolian family. Her mother Althaia, notorious in myth for the murder by magic of her son Meleager, is never mentioned, nor is Meleager himself, the famous hunter of the Kalydonian boar and the killer of his uncles in battle. Even Deianeira's birthplace is arbitrarily changed from Kalydon to Pleuron,[4] as if to dispel the aura of violence that comes with her traditional Kalydonian context.

For savagery is something before which this Deianeira characteris-

---

3. "Apollodoros," *Library* I. viii. 1
4. Deianeira situates her family in Pleuron at line 7 of Sophocles' text. We have omitted the reference from the translation as an obscure geographical detail of no consequence for a modern audience.

tically retreats, as long as retreat is possible, to the safety of distance —as in her terrified withdrawal from the scene of Herakles' combat with Achelöos (509ff)—or to the shelter of the marriage bed, the symbol of her hopes for security and the site of her nocturnal fears (103ff). She is, finally, the most timid of all Sophoclean protagonists, static and passive; her mode of survival is to wait danger out, to do nothing—or to try to do nothing.

In the prologue it is the Nurse who must provide her with the almost absurdly obvious remedy for her anxieties—to send out one of her children to find Herakles (56ff). Ultimately, however, the play illuminates the logic of this: throughout, Deianeira's thoughts thrust obsessively toward her own hearth, toward the security of family and home. Even the similes and metaphors she uses reflect her world of domestic values and concerns—a farmer visiting his fields (34ff), delicate plants protected from nature's violence (144ff), the dust falling from a saw (683), the ritual wine (686f). Similarly, the metamorphoses explicitly worked upon her by the poetry of the play give no hint of violence; she is a helpless bird (105), a frightened calf (516).

In the end, of course, Sophocles brings her to discover the tragic truth, the same lesson which the poet's contemporary Thucydides read in human history: that the forces of savagery, though temporarily dormant or concealed, never entirely disappear from the civilized world. At the very moment when she believes that Herakles' final victory has shut these forces out, they march in upon her in the person of Iole, the silent token of her husband's brutality and lust, penetrating the palace itself and striking at Deianeira's citadel—her marriage bed. Passive withdrawal is no longer possible; her deliverer is now himself the source of danger. This is the moment of crisis which sparks the recollection that for years she has had with her, safely confined in a dark corner of her house, the essence of that same fearful power which permeates her husband's world: the poisoned blood of Nessos.

Deianeira's moment of equivocation (565ff) reflects the desperate deflection of simple caution and civilized conscience required by her decision to use this force as a love-charm. But she is soon disabused of her delusion. The omen of the wool drives her to acknowledge the danger implicit in her action, and Hyllos arrives to confirm her fear: she has unloosed something more savage than the lust she wanted to "tame" (643f). The "charm" by which she hoped to attach her husband's affections has struck—and stuck—"like venom from a snake" (754). She can only wilt and, in another cruel irony, "crawl" away into the palace to find, in suicidal violence, her final escape from brutality (798ff). There she reaffirms her lifelong dream of domestic peace, carefully making up the marriage bed and slaughtering herself upon it: dead wife dutifully awaiting the return of the dying husband (892ff).

III

Herakles was rarely portrayed as a sympathetic hero by the Greek tragedians.[5] In his nature there was, in addition to an occasional element of buffoonery, a brutishness which made him singularly unsuited for heroic treatment. In this play, however, this very trait is an asset and is incorporated, with all its raw vitality, as an integral part of Sophocles' design. Herakles here is the embodiment of all that is antithetical—and ultimately inimical—to the world of civilized constraint which Deianeira tries to shape. He belongs to a world of limitless space, the vast landscape against which the Chorus pictures him in the parodos, a lonely figure "spinning" on the troubled seas of his life (116ff). It is a world of "woods / and seas" (970f), inhabited by forces of inhuman savagery: man-eating lion; Hydra; monstrosities, half-men, half-horse; wild boar; three-headed whelp of the Viper; and watchful dragon (1040ff).

His heroic mission—the endeavor which earns him the epithet of "the greatest man who ever lived" (173; 797)—has been to overpower these forces by sheer strength. It is a particularly primitive form of heroism, not self-chosen but imposed, a kind of licensed exercise of savagery which is distinguishable from the bestial elements it destroys only because it claims to serve civilization's purpose. From the beginning humanity has required such champions—and found them, to its ruin as well as to its salvation, in those men of obsessive violence represented by the Herakles of this play.

Here the hero is revealed as a figure of crushing strength, uninhibited by the constraints of conscience and family loyalty which bind Deianeira to the civilized world. Serenely he offers up to Zeus the spoils of a city pillaged by his lust (733ff). He makes no effort to conceal from his wife his intention to replace her with the young captive he sends to be welcomed in her house (464ff). He is without compassion, maintaining stony indifference to Hyllos' anguish throughout

5. Of the three major tragedians, only Euripides is known to have attempted such a treatment. The successful result has fortunately been preserved in his *Herakles*.

the finale, just as he has earlier, in a chilling perversion of the conventional tragic gesture of self-sacrifice, compelled his son to risk death to rescue him (782ff). He murders Lichas despite the herald's denial of complicity in his ruin. The proof of Deianeira's innocent intentions evokes from him no word of pity or regret. Action means everything; motive, nothing. He remains, until his mysterious moment of enlightenment in the final scene, wholly preoccupied with the instrument rather than the aim of his heroic mission: with the once invincible body invoked in his hymn to his own epic achievement: "O hands, my hands . . . Shoulders . . . Chest . . . My arms . . . / Is it still you?" (1039f). All these he sees as incomprehensibly torn to shreds: "Pieces. Waste" (1053). Stripped of his muscle by a "weak, / meaningless woman" (1011f), he feels himself stripped of his manhood: "Look at me, / moaning, bellowing like a wispy girl . . . / Look! The hero! / All that time I was a woman!" (1021ff). The ravaging of his body has left him with nothing but a desire for an impossible revenge: "I might be nothing, / paralyzed in nothingness, but the one who did this / will know these hands . . ." (1057ff).

IV

What finally penetrates Herakles' blind obsession with his flesh, what restores his heroic spirit and frees him from despair, is the sudden discovery that his father Zeus has not betrayed him, that the oracular promises have, in fact, been fulfilled. Of these two oracles—one predicting that his release from toil would follow upon the sack of Oichalia (77ff; 163ff; 1119ff), the other that no living creature would be able to kill him (1107ff)—there are no traces in what survives of the mythical tradition from which Sophocles drew. It may well be that he has invented them; it is certain that he has included them to serve the tragic meaning of the action: to explain to the hero, and to the audience, why his career must at this time and in this way end.

It must end now, at the moment when Herakles has destroyed Eurytos' city, because that act in itself confirms a catastrophic shift in the focus of his energies. The violence of his spirit, which has been harnessed by civilization to attack its monstrous enemies, has broken rein; there is nothing left alive brutal enough to confront him with the threat of death, with genuine heroic challenge. And yet his thirst for savagery remains, seeking further victims—and finding them, as violent heroes too often have, in the very humans he once defended. The rampage of the beast can only be ended now by a kind of miracle, the resurrection from the dead of a former bestial adversary, by the resurrection, in other words, of his own heroic past. For the source of the poison which Nessos sends back to kill this murderer-rapist is in fact Herakles' own arrow, shot long ago at the same target: animal lust.

Sophocles does not have Herakles articulate this meaning after he senses the coherence of his destiny. This would be not only out of character but also dramatically superfluous; for by this point the special logic underlying the oracular ambiguities of the play has already revealed its meaning.

The development of this logic is initiated at the very beginning of the play by emphasis on certain disturbing changes in the pattern of Herakles' behavior. Deianeira's deliverer, civilization's heroic servant (36ff), has turned murderer and found service of a shockingly different sort. He has "killed poor Iphitos" (41); the poet needed to have Deianeira say nothing more, for the atrocity of this crime had already been told in Homer's Odyssey (XXI. 1ff). And when Hyllos reports the sequel to this murder, "slavery" to a barbarian woman, his mother is astonished: "If he stood for that, then anything is possible" (72).

But this subservience to barbarism is only the ominous prelude to Herakles' complete rejection of the constraint upon which his claim to heroism is founded. The servitude to Omphale is over. The hero's savagery has become its own master—and we are confronted with the results: with the miserable victims of his latest triumph (212ff), with Lichas' brain-splattered death (762ff), and, finally, with the spectacle of Herakles himself consumed by violence. The Chorus in the third stasimon has foreseen the truth: for a man like Herakles, escape from the limitations of servitude is inevitably linked to the death of the heroic spirit: "Because how, how would the empty-eyed, the see-nothing, / still have work, toil to do, / bondage, if he's dead?" (813ff).

Herakles has succumbed to the monstrous world in which he has lived; he has become, in fact, another Nessos. This transformation is underscored throughout the play by images of animal violence. In Deianeira's account of the combat with Achelöos the outlines of man and monster remain distinct (9ff). But later, when the Chorus takes up the theme in the first stasimon, the distinction begins to blur: the conflict ends in a confusion of identities, a battle of bulls over a calf (502ff). Immediately thereafter, Deianeira sends the gift which her husband is to open "when he makes the bull-kill" (593) and which reduces him to the thrashing, eye-rolling, bellowing beast described by Hyllos in the following scene (770ff). Horrified, the Chorus articulates the ghastly image of Herakles "fused to the spirit / of the Hydra" (821f). First bull, then snake: the hero has become indistinguishable from Acheloös. (Cf. 9ff.) In the finale these images find their culmination. The hero is at last brought before the audience, tortured by an invisible and inescapable monster. "Driving teeth," "pouncing, lunging . . . leaping, destroying," Herakles' bestialized nature has, in the end, recoiled upon itself (945; 984f).

V

Of all the many changes enacted in the world of *Women of Trachis*, this is the most devastating: the greatest man who ever lived is reduced to a shrieking woman. The play's climactic transformation, however, is still to come—in the reversal of Herakles' mood after he has perceived the accuracy of Zeus' oracles.

In an instant, all the rage and bitterness of his first cry to Zeus are gone. (Cf. 942ff.) Until this moment, Herakles has impotently struggled to escape his pain (957ff), lamenting the loss of his manhood. Now he proclaims Hyllos the physician he has despaired of finding: "healer . . . doctor . . . / Only you can cure this evil" (1158f). But it is the patient himself who specifies, with an icy assurance and an indomitable strength of will, his paradoxical treatment: death, fiery destruction on a pyre to be constructed with ritualistic precision (1146ff).

Sophocles refuses any explicit clarification of this change. On the contrary, he stresses the uncanniness of the hero's recovered confidence through Hyllos' unanswered pleas for explanation. Instead the answer has been left beneath the surface of the dialogue, in the shape of the action itself. Herakles, after the vindication of his father's oracular word, seems to find liberation in a meticulously prescribed pattern of behavior. The inference is irresistible that the source of this prescription is in these same oracles, or, more precisely, in certain unspecified aspects of these privileged communications between Herakles and Zeus.

Sophocles has clearly hinted that these oracles are more than the usual Olympian edicts issued by a detached divinity. Early in the play he refers to them as "covenants" (*ksunthēmata*: 156), a word suggesting a kind of contract, struck by mutual consent and defining mutual obligations carefully inscribed, in good Greek legal fashion, on a tablet. And it is precisely this peculiar contractual aspect of the oracles which is reinforced by the superficially strange behavior of the hero at the end. The fulfillment of Zeus' word has made binding the pact which the son thought broken by his father's betrayal; at once Herakles initiates the execution of his own obligations: self-immolation upon Mt. Oita. As he does so, moreover, the nature of this unstated confrontation between Zeus and hero is revealed by the parallel confrontation between Herakles and Hyllos. Herakles demands from his son no less than Zeus has demanded of him, blind obedience to the paradoxical commands of an implacable father: "You ought to know at your age that obedience / to the father is the most important law" (1127f).

Such mystification, extraordinary for a Greek tragedian, can only be explained by Sophocles' determination to mark the change in Herakles for what it is: a miracle, a transformation possessed of no logic communicable to common mortals, its origins obscured in secrets between demigod and divine father. Zeus' son confronts the revelation that his ultimate adversary is his own ferocity, that his body, which has been the instrument of his triumphs, has in the end been the instrument of his defeat; and he finds in unprotesting acceptance of this paradox a new source of strength. As he leaves the stage it is no longer his ruined body which he invokes, but rather his spirit, directed now to reaffirm the forgotten heroic task by curbing the beast which has broken rein: "Soul, be hard now! . . . / Put the steel bit in your teeth" (1208f). With this metaphor Herakles departs to complete the sacrificial ritual which has been interrupted by Deianeira's gift—the triumphant bull-kill in which the celebrant has himself become the consummating victim.

The hero is convinced that the outcome of this "welcome, unwelcome work" must be "joy" (1212f). To find cause for jubilation in self-destruction is to transcend the limits of mortal vision. Herakles has been transformed from something less than human into something more than hero, an austere god-figure, enforcing his inexplicable will with pitiless compulsion and confronting the future with omniscient assurance. Here, surely, lies the reason why so many critics have failed to find in him the sympathetic hero conventional to Sophoclean tragedy. Men, not savages or gods, move audiences to pity.

It is far more for Hyllos, the surviving son, than for Herakles that the close of Women of Trachis evokes compassion. Here the untroubled youth of the opening scene becomes a man. His father, with the indifference of life itself, compels him to accept the justice (1194f) of a world where killing is cure and marriage to the instrument of a mother's ruin a filial obligation. For those who live there can be no escape from violence. Hyllos must live with the knowledge that he has been an accomplice in his father's death; and he will be bound to Iole, a permanent reminder of the savagery which has destroyed his parents. In this enforced submission to inexplicable realities he, unlike his father, can find no joy but only bitterness. He is, after all, not a son of Zeus.

The austerity of the tragedy's climactic vision contrasts strikingly with the optimism of Sophocles' last play, Oedipus at Kolonos. There, too, mystery and paradox play critical roles. Oedipus, like Herakles, possesses a "covenant" (ksunthēma: 46) with a god, Apollo. He has been assured that upon reaching the Grove of the Furies at Athens he will be released from his life as a blind pariah and transformed into a sacred hero with eternal powers to help his friends and harm his enemies. At the end of the play this divine promise is realized in the spectacle reported by the Messenger: thunder rolls, the voice of "heaven" is heard, and Oedipus is miraculously spirited out of sight.

Sophocles could easily have used a similar means to refute Hyllos' closing cry of protest and to confirm the Chorus' stubborn faith in the benevolence of Zeus toward his children (138f). He needed only to appropriate the happy ending already present in the myth. There, in the deification with which Herakles' self-destruction was rewarded, lay proof of the heroic spirit's capacity to survive its conflict with bestial impulse; to win eternal victory over death and change. Sophocles has encouraged his audience to expect such an ending, both by making Mt. Oita, the traditional site of Herakles' ascent to Olympos, a conspicuous feature of the play's landscape and by giving to the hero's instructions for his pyre suggestive overtones of religious ritual. But in the end Sophocles produces no stage divinity to confirm the crowning glory which awaits the hero. Instead, after opposing Hyllos' bleak vista of senseless human misery to Herakles' mysterious prospect of joy, he abruptly ends the play with no suggestion of a final resolution; without so much as the conventional closing word from the Chorus.

It is from this suspension of final judgment that Women of Trachis derives its stunning tragic impact. Through it the poet compels us to share the pain of Hyllos' confrontation with a divine justice which transcends the logic of human experience. Such justice is, by definition, unknowable; and Sophocles, by his pointed refusal to realize the apotheosis, proclaims his unwillingness to provide the comfort of any illusion to the contrary. Hyllos assumes the burden of unquestioning faith in his father as the price for his escape from despair. Herakles departs to die, stifling all impulse to mourn his end —confident that the unwelcome will become welcome, that defeat will become victory. But Sophocles has made the finality of his triumph a matter of agonizing doubt. Ajax and both Oedipus plays clearly affirm mankind's capacity to transcend impermanence by heroic moral courage. For the problem he has addressed in Women of Trachis Sophocles offers no such certain answer. The possibility of humanity's ultimate victory over inherent savagery is no more than a bright, unrealized hope. There is but one certainty in the unpredictable universe of this play. It is affirmed at the end by Hyllos: ". . . nothing is here, / nothing, / none of all of it, that is not Zeus" (1225ff).

VI

In view of the lack of firm evidence it is impossible to feel much conviction in assigning Women of Trachis even an approximate date. The attempt to establish its dependence on Euripides' Alcestis of 438 B.C. seems at best inconclusive. About all that can safely be said is that the play can be shown to possess, in its vocabulary and technique, certain affinities with Ajax and Antigone, both generally thought to be the earliest of the seven surviving Sophoclean tragedies. This would suggest a production around 440 B.C., in the middle years of the poet's career.

As the basis of our translation we have used the text of R. C. Jebb, Sophocles: the Plays and Fragments: Part V: The Trachiniae (Cambridge, 1892). Occasionally (at 643-5, 825-9, 885, and 890) we have preferred the manuscript tradition to the emendations accepted in his edition, and in one instance (201-4) we have adopted the reading of A. C. Pearson's Sophoclis Fabulae (Oxford, 1955).

We are grateful to the many who have encouraged and assisted us throughout our collaboration. Our specific debts have been separately acknowledged at the close of the Translator's Comments and the collaborating scholar's Notes.

Bryn Mawr, Pennsylvania   GREGORY W. DICKERSON

Philadelphia, Pennsylvania   C. K. WILLIAMS
April 15, 1975

WOMEN OF TRACHIS

CHARACTERS

HERAKLES hero of the famous labors, the son of Zeus
DEIANEIRA his wife
HYLLOS their son, approaching manhood
NURSE
LICHAS Herakles' herald
MESSENGER
OLD MAN
CHORUS of young women of Trachis
LEADER of the Chorus
CAPTIVES young women of Oichalia
IOLE one of them, the daughter of Eurytos
SERVANTS

Line numbers in the right-hand margin of the text refer to the English translation only, and the Notes at p. 79 are keyed to these lines. The bracketed line numbers in the running headlines refer to the Greek text.

Dawn.

The palace of Keyx, king of Trachis. Massive doors. To one side, a statue of Zeus, with an altar.

Enter from the palace, DEIANEIRA. *Behind her and unseen by her, the* NURSE.

DEIANEIRA Men have been telling each other since time
started: if you're going to say happy or unhappy
about a human life, wait for it to be over.
Me, though, my life—I don't need Hell to teach me
the turns in my life or how much it weighs.
Even when I still lived at home with my father
Oineus . . . Girls are afraid of marriage,
you're supposed to be. I was a girl, but nobody
ever felt the ice I felt. There was a river.
His name was Achelöos, and it was that,   10
a river, *that,* who wanted me. My father
would see shapes. I was being wooed by shapes!
There'd be a torrent of a bull, it would be him,
then a snake, coiled and shimmering—him—
then something with the face of an ox, a man's body
and a thick beard gushing jets of water.
Again, him. I'd look at him—my admirer—
and I used to pray to die if they brought me
anywhere near a bed with a thing like that in it.

Then finally Herakles arrived. I soared!   20
The famous Herakles. Alkmene's child, the son of Zeus.
He faced the other, fought him, I was saved.
If you want to know about the battle itself,
ask someone who wasn't paralyzed, who wasn't ice,
who didn't sit there overwhelmed with the dread
that my own beauty was going to spin curses for me.
However it did happen, though, the part of god
who watches these war things made it come out right . . .

17

If right really is right, because ever since I've been
with Herakles, sharing his bed, standing with him,   30
all I seem to have done is nurse terror for him.
One night is fear, the next drives that fear out
with new fear.
           We had children, of course.
He sees them the way a farmer sees his back fields:
he drops a seed and comes around once in awhile
to check the harvest.
            All right, that was his life,
home, gone, home and then slogging away again
to labor for some master or another. But now
he's supposed to have risen above all that
and now my anxieties are worse than ever.   40
He killed poor Iphitos and we've been uprooted since,
exiled in Trachis, the guests of people
we hardly know and where is he? Tell me.
All I know is that he's disappeared again
and that I'm being torn to bits for him again.
And it's been so long this time . . . ten months . . .
no, five more even than that and not a word.
What kind of trouble will it be this time?
He gave me something to keep for him
when he left, a tablet. I only hope   50
it doesn't mean more suffering for me.

The Nurse comes forward and addresses DEIANEIRA.

NURSE Queen . . . Deianeira . . . I've watched you for such a
        long time
groaning and carrying on about Herakles being away.
I've never said a word: you are the Queen
and I the slave. Would you forgive me now
if I suggested something? You have so many children—
why haven't you ever sent one of them to search
for your husband? Hyllos is old enough. Why not?
Look, he's running home right now.
If it doesn't bother you that it's my idea,   60
why don't you use it and him along with it?

Enter HYLLOS, *returning from a game or hunt, running.*

DEIANEIRA Son, sweetheart, good advice
can come from anyone, apparently. This woman's
my slave, but you'd never know from what she says.

HYLLOS What advice, Mother? Am I allowed to hear?

DEIANEIRA Shouldn't you be ashamed, she says, all this time,
never trying to find where your father is?

HYLLOS But I know where he is, or I hear rumors, anyway.

DEIANEIRA What rumors? What are you talking about? Where?

HYLLOS All last year, they say, he was a slave in Lydia,   70
to a woman; some barbarian. The whole year, he ploughed.

DEIANEIRA If he stood for that, then anything is possible.

HYLLOS Well, he's supposed to be out of it now.

DEIANEIRA Out of it where? Is he alive?

HYLLOS He's making war, they say, or getting ready to,
against Euboia, Eurytos' kingdom.

DEIANEIRA Son, listen to me. Don't you know about that place?
That he gave me prophecies about that place?

HYLLOS What kind of prophecies, Mother?

DEIANEIRA Important ones. They say: he dies, there, now.   80
They say: if he survives the there and now,
his labors will be over. What's left will be happiness,
peace and quiet for his life.
                              Hyllos, his future
is in the balance. Go help him. If he's safe,
so are we. If he's not, we're finished, too.

19

HYLLOS Mother, if I'd known about all this,
        prophecies like this, I'd be there now.
        With all the luck he's had, though,
        I didn't think we had to worry. About him,
        or anything. All right, I do know now.   90
        I'll find the truth, no matter what.

DEIANEIRA Go ahead, then. If news is good,
           it does good, late or not.

           Exit NURSE *into the palace. Exit* HYLLOS. *Enter* CHORUS.*

CHORUS   The night, the
                  shimmering night, is
                    slaughtered, her armor
                torn from her for you
                  to be unwombed and then she
                    beds you back in her, burning,
                on fire! SUN!
                  Listen!
                    You should know,
                Sun—listen!
                  The child,
                    the child of Alkmene,
                listen, where
                  is he, we're
                    asking, where, the child,
                is he?
                  O brilliance! O
                    fire-thing,
                in the sea-pit is   100
                  he?
                    On
                the doubled continents,
                  asleep—
                    is he there?

* The Chorus does not speak in unison. Each descending line is meant to be
spoken by a different voice. See Translator's Comments, p. 73.

Listen! Listen! You
   could see it! Eye-Lord!
      Seeing-Lord!
Because Deianeira, her,
   the heart-torn, o
      and she
was fought for, she,
   I've heard that she,
      her eyes,
like the blinded
   bird, the eyelids
      torn
with longing,
   never, never
      puts her
eyes
   away
      to sleep, not
dry, not dry, but nurses
   fear after
      fear for her husband,
his wanderings, and
   the obsessive bed,
      the widowed
bed,   110
   and doom,
      the
consuming,
   terrible, the
      expectation.

The sea! The
   sea! The way, look
      the way
the inexhaustible
   wind, look, sucks
      north
waves, south

waves, coming, look,
    coming
farther,
  endless,
    endless, so
Herakles, seed
  of Kadmos,
    so his life, that way,
one wave
  spinning it,
    another,
like the deep
  sea at Crete,
    swelling it
into labor.
  But listen, a god,
    one of them, the gods,
one of the knowers,   120
  always holds
    him
away, always, away
  from Hell, at least away
    from that house, always.

               They turn to DEIANEIRA.

And that's the reason
  I offer two mouths to
    you now,
for how you're acting.
  Respect, yes,
    but reproach, too, and
blame. Because you can't,
  no, shouldn't,
    no, never, mustn't,
ever, let
  hope, not all of
    hope, not

hope, erode.
    It wasn't
        painlessness
the all-King,
    all-Doer,
        Kronos-heir,
worked
    out for
        humanity. But
it circles,
    pain, it
        circles,
exaltation, to   130
    all, all
        of us,
like the Great
    Bear, the spinning,
        the spinning paths.

The shimmering
    night
        won't stay, wealth
won't,
    calamity
        won't, not
for humans won't
    at least, but
        suddenly, suddenly
it's disappeared,
    gone, and someone else,
        some poor else,
is under them; the
    joy, the
        deprivation.
I tell you,
    Queen,
        keep
that always, ever,

in your expectation.
Who, who
of anyone, has ever known
Zeus, not to think, the
.   god, of his children?

DEIANEIRA You must have heard about my suffering.   140
That's why you're here. But without being me,
you'll never understand it,
and may you never have to.
All the sweet things growing in their good places,
the sun's burning never touching them, or the rain or wind;
living their happy little joyfulness, until the virgin's name
is wife and then she knows anxiety and the night
and how to tremble for a husband and children.
Someone who's been through that could begin
to know me, what I'm living.   150
She'd look at her own troubles.
Well, I've done my share of crying until now, but now
I'm going to offer you a grief that's more
than all of them. Just before Herakles
was leaving on his latest journey, he gave me
an old tablet with strange covenants carved on it.
As many times as he'd gone out on trials before
he'd never bothered to explain anything—
he always left to conquer, not to die—
but this time it was as though he knew some doom   160
about himself. He told me how much of our property
was mine and what his sons should have
and he told me when: that if a year
and three months passed and he wasn't back,
then he'd be dead. Live that long, though,
and he could rest, from that day on.
He said it was ordained by the gods: the end
of the labors of Herakles. It's what the sacred oak
told him through the twin dove-priestesses
at Dodona . . . And the time is now, now,   170
so that every blessed night I come awake,

24

afraid that I'm a widow, that I'm deprived now
of the greatest man who ever lived.

LEADER Wait,
   quiet,
    doomed
or not doomed, no more
  words: someone
   with a wreath: that's joy.

Enter MESSENGER.

MESSENGER Queen Deianeira. Your humble servant, madam,
but with the news to liberate you from your unhappiness.
Not only is Herakles alive, he's won his war
and is bringing back spoils to give the gods.

DEIANEIRA What are you saying, old man? 180

MESSENGER That your hero husband will be home soon,
by your side, more powerful than ever.

DEIANEIRA Who told you that?

MESSENGER In the pasture, you know, where they take the oxen
in the summer? Lichas, the herald, is telling everyone.
As soon as I heard, I ran ahead to be the first
to tell you. I thought you might give me
a reward or at least your gratitude.

DEIANEIRA If it's such good news, why isn't Lichas here himself?

MESSENGER Why? Madam, it wouldn't be easy. 190
All the people have got him cornered, asking questions
and he can't move. They want to know
what's happened and they won't pass him on
until they do. He wants to come. They just won't let him.
But you'll see yourself. He'll be here soon.

25

DEIANEIRA O Zeus . . . your sacred meadows . . . the grass . . . Oita . . .
It had to be so long, but now, finally . . . finally . . .
All right, you, women, inside; you, out here, now,
everyone, cry out . . . Sing! . . . We are so glad. This
is beyond . . . the light of it . . . beyond . . . hope . . . joy!   200

                    The CHORUS, arms raised, dances.

CHORUS   SOAR!
                   LET THIS
                      HOUSE SOAR!
                HEARTH-
                   CRIES! HOUSE-
                   CRIES! ALTAR!
                The house!
                   The husband—
                      hungry house,
                let it
                   SOAR!
                      Men!
                To Apollo
                   soar!
                      His brilliant
                arrow! Women! The healing,
                   the healing-hymn, Apollo!
                      Healing!
                The hymn!
                   Soar!
                      Virgins!
                And for the
                   Sown-with-
                      him!
                The Sister!
                   Artemis!
                      Buck-
                Striker!   210
                   Double-
                      struck!

26

And the neighbor
　bride-
　　nymphs!

Their dance grows more and more abandoned. Enter LICHAS,
　　IOLE, *and the* CAPTIVES. *All but* LICHAS *are dishevelled,*
　　　　　　　　　　　　　　　　　　　　downcast.

CHORUS　　　Now watch
　　　　this! Watch
　　　　　this have me!
　　　　I'm letting it
　　　　have me!
　　　　　It has
　　　me! Look!
　　　　Soaring! ME!
　　　　　Can't think!
　　　JOY! ME!
　　　　Garlands!
　　　　　Now! The intoxicated
　　　now!
　　　　It's spinning!
　　　　　Whirling!
　　　RIGHT!
　　　　RIGHT
　　　　　HEALER!
　　　LOOK!
　　　　WOMAN!
　　　　　ANGEL!
　　　WHAT'S
　　　　CONFRONTING
　　　　　YOU! RIGHT NOW!
　　　LOOK! IT'S   220
　　　APPEARING!
　　　APPEARING!

DEIANEIRA　Here they are. Women, look:
　　　　could my eyes' look-out ever miss this march?

Wonderful, Lichas! Welcome! You took so long for someone
bringing joy . . . That is the right word, joy?

LICHAS It's good to be back and good to hear you welcome us,
Queen Deianeira. Your words suit your husband's triumph—
they are the right ones.

DEIANEIRA Wonderful man, tell me:
do I get Herakles back, alive?

LICHAS You do. I left him alive,   230
in good health, flourishing.

DEIANEIRA Where? Here or somewhere else?

LICHAS At Cape Kenaion, by the cliff. Consecrating
altars to his father Zeus and sacrificing.

DEIANEIRA Why? Is it only a vow he's fulfilling
or is there a prophecy?
LICHAS   A vow he made.

Before he took his spear against the country of these women.

DEIANEIRA And whose daughters are they . . . sad things?
Lord, unless I'm wrong, they should be pitied.

LICHAS They're Herakles' captives. He picked them out, for himself   240
and the gods, when he sacked Eurytos' city.

DEIANEIRA Is that the same war that kept him gone
until I couldn't count the days?

LICHAS It wasn't only that. Most of the time he was a captive
in Lydia, and not just a captive, and he admits
this himself, but a bought slave. Don't be upset
about the word "slave," though: it was god's work.
As I said, he admits he spent that year
in slavery to Omphale, the barbarian woman.

28

. But he was so furious about being disgraced that way   250
that he swore when his turn came he'd make a slave
himself out of the man who'd made it happen,
and out of the man's wife and child, too.
And he meant it. When he was finally freed,
he hired an army and went to Eurytos' city
because he said Eurytos was the only human being
who'd had any part in his misfortune. He'd been
Herakles' friend and when Herakles came to his house
and beat his sons at archery, he mocked him.
"My sons still could whip you . . . It was those damned,   260
magical arrows of yours, not you."
And then he called him a slave. "You're a slave,"
he said, "a free-man's lick-foot, and broken-down besides."
Then had him kicked out of the house
after dinner when he was drunk. That hurt.
Which must be why when Iphitos, one of the sons,
came to Tiryns one day looking for horses
and was thinking about something else, Herakles
took him and threw him from the tower. But Zeus,
Father of us all, King, wouldn't stand for him   270
killing by deceit that way,
even if it was the only time he did it. So he had him sold.
Bondage. Slavery. It wasn't the killing,
but the guile. If he'd done it openly, Zeus
would have pardoned the vengeance and called it justice,
victory. Anyway, the big-mouths, they're all in Hell
and their city's the slave now. These are their women,
pitiful, yes. They've lost the life they had
and here they are, with you. That's what your husband
wanted and, dependable, it's what I've done.   280
He'll be here soon himself, I'm sure. When he finishes
the sacrifices to his father. Of all my good news,
that must be the part that makes you happiest.

LEADER Queen . . .
         your joy . . .
               part

29

here, the rest
    promised . . .
        on the way . . .

                                DEIANEIRA *approaches the* CAPTIVES.

DEIANEIRA Of course. Isn't it just and right to rejoice
           in my husband's successes? God knows, I have reason to.
           The response should match the outcome, shouldn't it?
           Still, someone who thinks carefully about it
           might be afraid that someone's luck could turn   290
           and bring him to his knees. Friends, I feel
           so strangely sorry for these miserable orphans, homeless
           and fatherless in a foreign place. Women like this,
           they might have been rich men's daughters
           and now . . . slaves. Zeus, Tide-Turner,
           I hope you never touch a child of mine
           and if you do, let it be when I'm dead.
           That's what I'm afraid of, looking at these women.

           (*to* IOLE)

           You: who are you, poor woman? A virgin? A mother?
           You look so innocent . . . are you a princess?   300
           Lichas, whose daughter is this one?
           Who are her mother and father? Tell me . . .
           there's something about her . . . I feel sorrier
           for her than the rest. She seems to know
           what's in store for her.

    LICHAS Why ask me? How should I know? Maybe
           she's not the lowest of them, I don't know.

DEIANEIRA Could she be royal? Did Eurytos have a daughter?

    LICHAS I don't know. I didn't ask.

DEIANEIRA And you didn't hear her name from the others?   310

LICHAS   No, nothing. I didn't go into it.

DEIANEIRA   Poor thing.

(to IOLE)

If not Lichas, won't you tell me?
It's ridiculous not to know who you are.

LICHAS   It would be something if she talked now.
Let me tell you. Since we left, she hasn't said
a word, she just goes on and on moaning like an animal
about her disaster. The wind that raked us
on our way says more than she does.
It's hard for her, her silence is forgivable.

DEIANEIRA   Let her alone, then. She has enough pain.   320
I won't give her more. If it's what she wants,
she doesn't have to talk. Come, we'll go inside,
then you can start back when you want to.

LICHAS *and the* CAPTIVES *enter the palace.* DEIANEIRA *is about
to follow them but the* MESSENGER *touches her arm.*

MESSENGER   Wait! I have to tell you something.
You . . . not them . . .

(*Indicating* LICHAS *and the women*)

Let them go ahead.
I know things. You don't. You don't know anything
because nobody's told you anything and you should.

DEIANEIRA   What are you doing? Get out of my way.

MESSENGER   Wait, listen. You liked my first story,
maybe you'll like the next one better.   330

31

DEIANEIRA Should I call the others back? Or is what
you have to say only for my friends and me?

(*She indicates the* CHORUS)

MESSENGER You and them. Forget the rest.

DEIANEIRA They're gone now. Explain yourself.

MESSENGER That man, Lichas. He wasn't telling the truth
just now. Either that or he was lying before.

DEIANEIRA What are you saying? Don't give me riddles.
Tell me what you know.

MESSENGER I heard that same Lichas saying before—
and there were witnesses—that it was because of the girl   340
that Herakles destroyed Eurytos and his city.
If there was a god involved, it was Love
who fired him into making that war, Love,
not whatever happened in Lydia or being Omphale's slave
or killing Iphitos, however he did do it.
There's no Love in the story now, though,
is there? Supposedly, when Herakles
couldn't talk the father into giving him the girl
as his whore, he invented a pretext,
some petty complaint, and went to war against her country—   350
Eurytos ruled there, that much is true—
and murdered him and looted the city.
Look yourself. He doesn't casually send the girl
ahead with just anyone . . . and not to be a slave, don't
think that for a moment. He wouldn't dream of it,
not when he's on fire for her.
I thought I'd better tell you what I heard back there,
Queen Deianeira. There were a lot of others
who could convict him along with me;
he said it right in the main square of Trachis.   360
If what I say isn't welcome, I'm sorry.
But it's the truth, the whole truth, nothing but.

DEIANEIRA O my god. What's happening to me?
Have I been stabbed? What kind of thing
have I brought under my roof? My god.
He swore she doesn't have a name. Does she?

MESSENGER Yes, she's royal. In birth and name.
She's Eurytos' daughter and her name was Iole.
Lichas didn't know . . . remember? He never asked?

LEADER All the treachery   370
         there is,
             forget,
         compared to the monster
             who degrades himself
                 lying!

DEIANEIRA Women . . . Friends . . . What should I do?
I'm paralyzed . . . Tell me what to do!

LEADER Lichas:
         force him: make
             him answer.
         Maybe
             he'll give you what
                 you want.

DEIANEIRA I will. You're right. I will.

MESSENGER What about me? Do I wait, or what?

                                         Enter LICHAS from palace.

DEIANEIRA You stay. He's coming out of the house
on his own. I don't have to send for him.

LICHAS Deianeira, is there any message you want   380
to give to Herakles? I'm leaving now.

33

DEIANEIRA It took you so long to arrive and here you are
rushing off and we've hardly spoken.

LICHAS Is there more? Ask anything.

DEIANEIRA If I do, you'll give me the truth?

LICHAS I swear, by Zeus. Everything I know.

DEIANEIRA Then who's that woman you brought here?

LICHAS She's from Euboia. I don't know her family.

MESSENGER Hey, you, Lichas! Look at me. Who are you talking to?

LICHAS Who's this? How dare you speak like that to me?   390

MESSENGER Never mind. You understood. Just answer.

LICHAS To the royal Deianeira. Unless I'm seeing things.
Oineus' daughter, Herakles' wife: my Queen.

MESSENGER That's what I wanted you to say. Your Queen, right?

LICHAS Of course, my Queen. Just as it should be.

MESSENGER Aha! What kind of *just*-ice should you suffer then
if I can prove you're being unjust to her?

LICHAS Injustice? What is this nonsense?

MESSENGER Nothing. You're the one who's talking nonsense.

LICHAS I'm leaving. I was a fool   400
to listen to you in the first place.

MESSENGER No, you don't. Not till you answer one short question.

LICHAS All right, what is it? You'll tell me anyway.

MESSENGER That girl you brought, the slave. You know
who I mean?

(LICHAS *glances toward the palace*)

LICHAS   Of course, well?

MESSENGER Yes, right, that one back in there, the one you didn't know.
Didn't you say before . . . didn't you say
that she was Iole, Eurytos' daughter?

LICHAS Said where? Show me a witness who'll testify
to that, that he heard such a thing.   410

MESSENGER A lot of people heard you. In the square
at Trachis. The whole crowd.

LICHAS   Now, wait.
That's what I *said* I *heard*. But that was an opinion.
It's not the same as accuracy. Not strictly.

MESSENGER Strictly! Didn't you swear you brought her here
to marry Herakles?

LICHAS   Me? Marry?
For god's sake, Queen, who is this man?

MESSENGER Somebody who heard you say with your own lips
that Eurytos' city was destroyed out of love
for that girl. It wasn't the woman in Lydia   420
but Herakles' passion for the girl.

LICHAS Madam, get rid of this person. How can a sane man
argue with a lunatic?

DEIANEIRA Now, I'm going to beg you. In the name of Zeus,
of his bolts blasting the grass on his mountain Oita,
don't cheat me of my answer. Listen to me.

35

The woman you're talking to doesn't hold grudges.
I know what goes on with men, how things change,
how hearts change. The man's insane who tries to face
Love down, to go to blows with Love. Even the gods—   430
Love does what it wants to, even to them.
Do you think I'd expect a weak woman, me or anyone else,
to resist Love? I'd have to be mad to blame my husband
if he's sick for this girl. Or her. She can't hurt me.
Can I blame her? Never, impossible.
But if Herakles taught you to lie to me,
then you were low. And if you thought of it yourself
to keep from hurting me, you're lower still,
you're hurting me more. Just tell me the truth.
The brand of liar isn't worthy of you.   440
If you're thinking I won't find out what's happened,
don't. Too many heard who'll tell me anyway.
Are you afraid? That's absurd. *Not* to know,
that would cause me pain!
What's so terrible in knowing? Herakles
has loved more women than I can count—
did one of them ever have harsh words from me?
And neither will this one, no matter how
he's burning up for her. As soon as I saw her,
I felt compassion. As helpless and innocent   450
as she is and her beauty has still ruined her life
and enslaved her father's country. But all that's
waves in the wind, now. You, though: you lie
to someone else if you're going to lie, but not to me!

LEADER She speaks
          well,
                you'd do
     well
          to listen. You won't be
               sorry. We'll thank you, too.

LICHAS Deianeira . . . all right. I see you think
          the way we humans have to. We're weak.

36

I'll give you the truth, all of it.
It's just the way that one said it was.   460
Herakles' soul was driven through with desire
for the girl and he did do it because of her—
take his spear and go up against her father's city
and level it.
            But I have to be fair and tell you
that he never hid a thing and never asked
me to, either. I didn't want to hurt you,
so if there's a fault that way, it's mine.

Now you know what's been going on
but for your sake as much as for his,
let the girl be. Don't ever take back   470
what you said about her. His strength
has won so much for him but his passion
for this girl is more than he can master.

DEIANEIRA I realize. Don't trouble yourself.
I'm not going to make myself sick
fighting futile battles with gods.
Come, we'll go in. I'll tell you what message
to take to Herakles and give you gifts for him.
It wouldn't do to go back empty-handed
when you brought so much marching in.   480

Exit LICHAS and DEIANEIRA into the palace. Exit MESSENGER.

CHORUS   Some gigantic power,
                                    huge, is what
                                        Love, Love's goddess,
                                Love, always seems
                                    to wrench, always,
                                        from carnage.
                                I won't tell
                                    about the
                                        gods, not

37

them, how even they,
   with love, the gods, how
      even Zeus, Father
of Fathers, was taken
   in
      by her,
and Death,
   even
      he, Death
who owns night, even
   he was taken
      in by her
and even the whole
   earth, the
      Breaker . . .
But who was it,
   who,
      when they wanted this
woman, who was it   490
   who both
      went into combat, both,
heroes,
   into blows,
      heroes, the
grime, to
   the end, the final
      finish?

One was a river,
   Acheloös
      gigantic,
horns high!
   Power! Appearing!
   Power!
Disappearing!
   The bull, power, the
      brute! And the other,
Theban, from the

wine-country,
   bow-cocked,
spear, club-
   cocked, the
      breaker,
the son of
   Zeus, all
      his power.
They go in
   to find it, marriage
      in the heart
of it, the battle, and   500
   in it, heart of it, the
      battle, Love,
the goddess Love, the
   decider, her, her choosing
      wand, her wand.
Fist-
   crack! Bow-
      crack!
Then
   bull, then
      beast,
horn-
   crack, the
      swarming, the
confusion and then
   both,
      they were both,
both twisted, both
   strangling,
      groaning, both,
both
   groaning and
      groaning,
their faces
   broken, both,
      broken.

And she, all
    that while, she
        on her hill, in
the far distance, she   510
        gleaming, white,
            all in herself, frail,
she
    waited, waited
        there, husband-
waiting. And I
    can see it, I, and I,
        what I could tell
about that look of
    hers,
        that look, pitiful, they
both wanted, both
    needed, both,
        from her,
waiting, waiting, and
    then, suddenly,
        gone, she, suddenly she,
the calf, the calf torn,
    torn from its mother, bawling, gone,
        alone, lost, alone.

DEIANEIRA *enters from the palace, carrying a black casket*
with a seal.

DEIANEIRA Friends, our guest is still in there
saying goodbye but I had to slip out.
I want to tell you what my hands have done
and I want sympathy, too,   520
for what I'm suffering.
                    A virgin . . . no,
what virgin? A slut, cheap, outrageous trade,
has come into my house to weigh me down and now
we'll all spin under the same blanket.
That's the reward I have from Herakles,
my true, good love, for having taken care

of his home through all this miserable tim
Am I angry? I don't know how to be.
He's had the same infection often enough
But to have her here! To live with her,
to have to share him—can I stand for that?
And she's just blossoming. Men love pluckir
when they're like that. I'm on the path dowr.
drying up. Do you know what I'm afraid of?
That I'll be calling Herakles husband
but that child will be calling him to bed.

But no, I told you, anger is wrong for a wife.
I accept that. And besides,
I have a way to get us out of this.
When I was still a girl, one of the monsters   540
from the old time gave me something that I've kept
sealed in a bronze jar ever since. It was Nessos,
the centaur. I took the life's blood from his wound:
it was his dying present, the hairy animal!
He used to ferry people in his arms across a river;
no boat, no oars, no anything, just him.
When I first left home after my father
married me to Herakles, he was carrying me like that
and when we got to mid-stream, he put his hands on me.
I screamed. Herakles shot an arrow in him,   550
deep, through his chest, to the lungs.
As he was dying, Nessos started to talk to me.
"You're Oineus' daughter, aren't you?" he said.
"Since you're the last person I'll carry across here,
I'm going to give you something. Pay attention.
If you take a handful of the clots from my wound,
from where Herakles stained the arrow
with black poison from the blood of the Hydra,
you'll have a love-potion, a drug so strong
that Herakles would never look at another woman."   560

Well, I thought of all that now because after he died,
I did it: kept it, locked up, hidden.
And now I've impregnated this robe with it,

exactly the way his last words told me to.
It's done. I hate evil. I don't like
being obvious. I don't even like knowing about it
and I hate women who are that way . . .
But in this case, if charms or spells can defeat that girl,
can get Herakles back to me, then I'm ready . . . .
Unless I'm being rash . . . Do you think so?   570
Say so if you do . . . I'll stop . . . I will . . .

LEADER No, it
   seems
    all right
  to do
   if you think it can
    work.

DEIANEIRA I don't know for sure. He said
   it would. I can't tell till I try.

LEADER Then you
   have
    to
  try. No
   telling till
    you try.

          Enter LICHAS *from palace.*

DEIANEIRA We'll know soon enough. There's the man
   coming through the door. He'll be leaving soon.
   Only don't, ever, tell what I'm doing. No matter how shameful 580
   what's done in the dark is, at least it stays there.

LICHAS Well, Oineus' daughter, tell me what
   I should do. I'm late.

DEIANEIRA I was getting something ready, Lichas,
   while you were in there with those strangers.

This robe. I want you to take it to my husband
as a gift from me. My own hands wove it.
When you give it to him, I want you to tell him
that he has to be the first to wear it, no one else.
And that it mustn't be seen by the sunlight or   590
the firelight or even the altar-fire until he comes out,
shining, in front of everyone to show it to the gods
when he makes the bull-kill.
I promised myself once that if he came home safe
and sound, I'd wrap him in it
and offer him reverently to the gods
like a newborn child, to be their sacrificer.

Here's my sign, set in the circle of my seal.
He'll recognize it. Now go.
But don't forget this time, you're a messenger,   600
keep out of it, don't meddle.
Do it right. We'll thank you, both of us,
he and I . . .

LICHAS Don't worry.
I'm not going to fall on my face.
I'll get it to him
and your exact words, too.

DEIANEIRA Goodbye, then. You know how things are
with us here.

LICHAS   Everything's well, I know.
I'll tell him.   610

DEIANEIRA   And you'll tell him
how I greeted the girl, that I welcomed her?

LICHAS I was amazed by that, and moved . . . yes.

DEIANEIRA There's nothing more. I'm afraid
to say how much I miss him
until I'm sure it's the same there.

43

Exit LICHAS, *with the casket.*

CHORUS

O, anyone,
  anyone who lives
    by the harbor, anyone,
by the rocks,
  the boiling
    streams, the crags;
who lives
  by Oita, the mountain,
    lives
by the sea
  that sits in land or by
    the shore
the Huntress-Goddess   620
  owns,
    the golden-arrowed
one: you know
  where,
    where the Greeks
hold council, where
  the gates
    are . . .

All of you, listen,
  you'll hear
    it soon, soon,
the flute-voice, the
  life,
    the sweet life-music . . .
O, gorgeous,
  not the hard, death-
    wail, the
wailing but sweet,
  godly and soft, like
    strings, strings.
Because the son
  of the woman
    Alkmene, the son

of Zeus, the god-son, is
rushing, the hero,
rushing, huge,
home, rushing
home,
with treasure.

He was gone   630
so long, so
long disappeared
from here, so
long, twelve months,
twelve, waiting.
He spun,
the sea,
we knew
nothing, nothing, and
the darling
wife, darling
sufferer,
wretch, the
heart-torn,
torn . . . She . . .
she was perishing, she,
every moment.
But now!
Now and now! the stung-
mad
war-god, now, has let
it be unleashed, the day,
the day!

O let him,
let him get
here! Here! Let
the oars not
stop, never
stop, not

until
  he gets
    here, not.
Let him leave
  that island, island-
    fires,
leave the
  sacrifice he's
    doing
and get here, get
  here, get here,
    here, tamed, finally,
tamed, soothed, with
  the robe, the ointment,
    soothed, soothed,
fused
  with it, the way the
    beast prescribed it.

DEIANEIRA *enters from palace.*

DEIANEIRA Friends . . . Everything I did . . . my act . . .
          I'm afraid I've gone too far!

LEADER Deianeira,
          Daughter of Oineus,
            What?

DEIANEIRA I don't know, but I have a premonition
          that what I did in good faith is turning evil.

LEADER Is it Herakles'
          gift? Is it
            that?

DEIANEIRA Yes, that. Listen to me.
          If you have to act in the dark, don't act.

LEADER Tell us,
        you're afraid . . . of
           what?

DEIANEIRA Without my telling you, you wouldn't dream
        what happened. You couldn't conceive it.
        The thing I used to smear the ointment on the robe,
        a ball of sheep's wool: it vanished!
        And nothing in the house consumed it—it devoured itself,
        wasted and corroded itself on the pavement.   660
        Wait. Let me tell you everything, all of it.
        I didn't leave out anything that beast the centaur,
        as he was writhing and dying with Herakles' arrow
        burning in his side, told me:
        it was bitten into my memory
        like a law on a bronze tablet.
        He ordered. I obeyed . . .
        To keep the drug in a dark, secret place
        away from fire, even away from the warmth of sunlight
        so I'd have it fresh when I was ready.   670
        And that's what I did. It was the time.
        Now. I was alone.
        I did the anointing with a tuft of wool
        I pulled from one of our sheep and then I folded
        the robe and put it in a casket
        to be out of the light . . . You saw that . . .
        But when I went back in, I saw—o god,
        how can I believe myself? . . .
        Somehow I happened to throw the used fleece
        into a patch of blazing light—sunlight—   680
        and when it was warm, it shrivelled up and fell
        apart on the ground into a kind of powder
        that looked like the dirt a saw cutting wood makes.
        That's still there. But underneath, where it fell,
        clots of hot foam have boiled up
        the way the earth on a grave boils when you pour
        the dark wine of Dionysos on it.
        What can I think now?

I've done something hideous!
That monster: why, in thanks for what,   690
should he do kindnesses for me
when his dying was my fault?
O no! He was lying to me! Using me!
He wanted to get back at his killer.
I understand it now, now, when it's too late.
Unless I'm wrong, it's me, o god, me,
who's going to kill my husband.
Of course! The arrow
that wounded him even hurt Cheiron, and Cheiron
was a god! Whatever living thing it can touch, it kills!   700
And if it's the same poison that oozed black
out of the centaur's wounds,
how can it not kill Herakles? I'm afraid
it will, it will.
                        But I've decided. If he falls,
I go with him. I die, too. How could a woman
who believed in her goodness the way I did
go on living if her name meant infamy?

LEADER You're right
            to be afraid but
                don't
        give
            away too soon your
                hope.

DEIANEIRA If the trying was evil in the first place,   710
           why keep courage with false hope?

LEADER But they'll
            believe, you didn't
                know.
        Who could be angry when
            you didn't
                know?

48

DEIANEIRA That's innocence. You did
no evil, what do you know?

Enter HYLLOS.

LEADER You'd better hush . . .
unless you want your son to know.
He's found his father; they're here.

HYLLOS Mother, I wanted one of three things when I came here.
That I'd find you dead. That you wouldn't be my mother
anymore. Or that you'd be another person altogether,
with somebody else's heart inside you.   · 720

DEIANEIRA Hyllos! What have I done to make you hate me?

HYLLOS I'll give you what! The man, your husband, yes,
my father—him—you've slaughtered him!

DEIANEIRA Son, my god, what's coming out of you?

HYLLOS Truth. What has to be.
Who can undo the done?

DEIANEIRA What are you saying, Child? It's monstrous!
On whose authority can you accuse me?

HYLLOS My authority! I saw it! My eyes!
His agony . . . His fall . . .   730

DEIANEIRA Where did it happen? Were you by his side?

HYLLOS If you want to know, I'll tell you. All of it.
After he sacked Eurytos' city, he left
with the spoils, the first-fruits of what he'd won.
There's a sea-cliff at Euboia called Cape Kenaion.
He set up altars there and dedicated a grove
of sacred trees to his father, Zeus, and that's

49

where I found him. I loved him then. O I loved him.
Just as he was starting the sacrifice,
Lichas, his own messenger, came   740
and brought your gift, that murderous robe.
And he put it on, the way you said he should,
and began the killing. Twelve giant bulls,
the best he'd won. And more, a hundred
altogether; everything that was brought to the altar,
big and small. And he was so serene at first,
unsuspecting; so proud of that robe, so happy in it.
But when the bloody fires started blazing
with the pine tar and the dripping fat, sweat
suddenly bubbled up on his flesh and the robe embraced him,   750
clung to his sides, at every joint
as though somebody'd soldered it on. And then
a gnawing seemed to start on his bones, convulsing him,
eating at him like venom from a snake.
He shouted for poor Lichas, who'd had nothing to do
with it, and asked him why he'd brought that robe,
what kind of scheme did he have in mind?
But Lichas didn't know anything. He could only say
what you told him to say; that the robe was a gift
from you. When Herakles heard that,   760
a spasm of pain seemed to shoot into his lungs
and he grabbed Lichas by the foot, right
where the ankle pivots in the socket and just
threw him at a rock sticking out of the water.
His head shattered. The brains erupted
through his hair and blood and pieces of the skull.
Everyone in the crowd was shrieking with horror.
One was insane, the other dead,
but nobody dared come near him
because he kept throwing himself onto the ground   770
and leaping, howling and screaming, into the air
until the rocks were ringing from the mountains
at Lokris all the way back to the cliff at Euboia.
But when he couldn't move anymore, when he was too
exhausted with hurling himself

into the dirt and lay there on the ground,
groaning, cursing you, his marriage with you—you, vile!—
and cursing ever dealing with your father and ruining
himself, then he lifted up out of the shrouds
of smoke—his eyes were rolling in his head—   780
and picked me out where I was crying in the crowd.
And called to me. "Son, come here! Don't run away
from my pain. Even if you have to die
my death with me, don't. Get me out of here!
Put me someplace where I can't be seen,
or if you're too soft for that, at least
take me out of this country so I won't die here."
He didn't have to ask again. We put him
on our ship and brought him, or what was left of him,
the bellowing, the torment, and landed him here.   790
And you'll see him soon, just alive, or just dead.
These are the things, my Mother,
you've plotted, and executed, and been caught at.

I hope punishing justice finds you. I hope the Furies
pay you back. I pray for it and it's right.
I know it's right because you've crushed the right—
you've destroyed the greatest man who ever lived.

> DEIANEIRA *starts toward the palace.*

LEADER   Don't crawl
    away! Speak! Your
      silence . . .
You're pleading
    for the
      prosecution.

HYLLOS   Let her crawl! Let a gale blow up   800
    to crawl her out of my sight!
    Mother! The name mother in her—
    it's a miscarriage.

No, let her crawl off in her rejoicing
to find the same joy she's given my father.

Exit DEIANEIRA *into the palace. Then* HYLLOS.

CHORUS   O children, look, children,
                                 look how suddenly, suddenly,
                                     it's come breaking
                             on us, the word,
                                 the god-
                                     word
                             out of the old-
                                 time, the prophecy
                                     from the old-time.
                             It shrieked. It
                                 shrieked that when the twelve
                                 years, the twelve
                             ploughing-times with   810
                                 them, the turning
                                     over of years, that then
                             the labor of the son, the
                                 son of Zeus, would
                                     end, and it's
                             accurate, exact,
                                 it's sailed, crashed,
                                     thundered, in on us.
                             Because how, how
                                 would the empty-eyed, the see-
                                     nothing,
                             still have
                                 work, toil
                                     to do,
                             bondage,
                                 if he's
                                     dead?
                             Because,
                                 because, if the murderous
                                     cloud, the venomous, clinging,

52

obscure cloud of
   the centaur-beast's eternal
     venom,
that came from death,
   nursed in the shimmering
    of the serpent,
if that's what
   stings
     him, his sides,
then how will he ever,   820
   ever, see another
    sun than this;
this man, only
   man, fused
    to the spirit
of the Hydra?
   The words
    themselves,
the words of the black-haired
   beast themselves,
    jumbled, obscure,
must seem themselves to
   be prodding, into
    him, boiling him themselves.

And none of this, none
   of it, the poor
    being, the woman, the
relentless, gigantic
   ruin, she saw none, impending
    for her family, none,
the new
   marriage bearing down . . .
    What would happen? Could
she know what would come
   from the beast-
    word,
the intercourse?

O,
 O, she must
be bellowing   830
  with this, groaning
    hideously with
this,
 moaning,
   dissolving,
new tears, the
  dew, pervading,
   new tears . . .
And DOOM
  is coming
    and DOOM,
revealed, obscure again,
  gigantic,
    ruins . . . ruins . . .

An eruption . . .
  it must be an explosion!
   Hot tears!
An infection
  has poured down
    through the
other, the him, worse
  than any enemy, any, with
    hands, ever inflicted,
worse than anything Herakles
  suffered
   that we would give
pity for. The spear,
  the point,
    gored, victorious,
point, you brought   840
  this
    bride
so quickly
  didn't you? Quickly
    from the mountains

of Oichalia . . .
     and Love . . .
          and Love . . .
     the servant
     Love,
          the silent, the
     obedient, all that time
          was the avenger! Maker!
          Made these things!

(A low, continual groaning is heard from
the palace: HYLLOS)

LEADER Is that imagination
     or
          did somebody
     groan inside
          that house? Is
          it pity? What
     now? What
          can I say now? It's no
          illusion . . .
     Another
      wail of
          misfortune
     for that
          house. More
          Pain.
     Look, the   850
          old
               woman,

                    The NURSE enters from the palace.

     her face . . .
          what is she
               bringing? News?

NURSE Women . . . Daughters . . . the endless sorrow
     that gift to Herakles has loosed.

55

LEADER Talk,
    woman, a new
      calamity?

NURSE Deianeira has disappeared . . . her last journey . . .
    without a single step.

LEADER You don't
    mean . . . not
      death?

NURSE You heard.

LEADER Death? Her?
    Pitiable
      her?

NURSE You heard. Again.   860

LEADER The lost
    soul lost.
      How?

NURSE Horribly. Horribly.

LEADER Woman, tell
    us, how
      did her doom come?

NURSE Her own hand. She finished it herself.

LEADER What rage
    she must have
      had! What frenzy!

NURSE A point. A weapon.

LEADER Alone?
    Death upon death and
      alone?

56

NURSE Steel. Freezing steel.

LEADER But you were
      there, fool;
          did you stand and watch?

NURSE I was there . . . I watched . . . I was there . . .   870

LEADER How did it happen? How
      did it happen? How
          did . . .

NURSE Her own hand . . . herself . . .

LEADER WHAT?
      WHAT?
          WHAT?

NURSE True.

LEADER The bride, the upstart,
      has given birth to giant
          Fury for this house.

NURSE You're right. If you were there
      to see it, you'd feel the pity even more.

LEADER Hands . . .
      A woman's hands . . .
          Could they?

NURSE They could, o yes, awful, yes they could.
      I'll tell. When she came into the house—she was alone—   880
      and saw her son making a litter up
      in the courtyard to bring his father in,
      she hid herself where no one could see her
      and then she fell on the altar, bellowing

that she was alone now, moaning . . . And when she'd touch
something she used to use, any old domestic thing,
the angel, before all this, she'd cry,
and if she met one of her servants, she'd cry again,
angel again, then cried that she was doomed,
no children anymore, nothing, for all time.   890
Then she suddenly stopped, all of it,
and I saw her rush into Herakles' room—she didn't know
I was watching, she couldn't see me—
and made the bed, her husband's bed,
and fell in it and dissolved in a burst
of brilliant tears. And talked to it.
"Dear bed . . . my dearest love-bed . . . Dear room,
       love . . .
You'll never welcome me again . . . Goodbye!"
And then was quiet. And with a violent spasm
tore her robe where it was pinned with a gold brooch   900
so that her left side and her arm were bare
and I ran as fast as I could to warn the son
but before we could get there she'd plunged a war-sword
into herself . . . into the side, where life lives.
The son shrieked when he saw it.
He'd learned from someone in the house, poor child,
but it was too late, that she'd acted
unintentionally,
that she'd only obeyed the word of the beast.
And he knew his rage had made her   910
do the thing. He kneeled, howling,
shattered, and kissed her
on the mouth and lay down side by side with her,
crying that he'd murdered her with slander,
crying again that he had to live his life
with no father and no mother now . . . an orphan.
And that's where it is inside this house.
Anyone who tries to see two days ahead
or more, is mad.
There's no tomorrow at all   920
until the day we're in is suffered through.

58

Exit NURSE *into the palace. Enter* HYLLOS *from the palace with* SERVANTS *carrying the litter. It is of heavy, rough-hewn wood. The bed-planks, at waist-height, are strewn with skins and hides.* HYLLOS *and the* SERVANTS *exit.*

CHORUS   Who groan for
                           first? Which is the worse disaster?
                                 Where begin? Misery.
                     Look, there's
                           one; we're waiting, there's
                                 another. Pain, waiting, it's the same.
                     I wish a breeze would come
                           blasting out of the hearth
                                 to carry me from here.
                     I'm afraid I'll die
                           of terror, of terror, to suddenly
                                 look at the son of Zeus,
                     the giant, because he's coming
                           now, in incurable torment, a wonder
                                 of unspeakable sorrowing.

                     Enter HYLLOS, *the* SERVANTS, HERAKLES *on
                     the litter. He is unmoving, eyes closed. An*
                                       OLD MAN *is with them.*

                     It's right here,
                           now, then, what I was crying like
                                 a nightbird for. Strangers. Coming.
                     How are they
                           bringing him? Sorrowfully.
                                 Adoringly. Mournfully.
                     Silently.
                           Oh, it is he! And he's
                                 silent. Is he dead? Sleeping?

HYLLOS O my god.   930
               Father . . . my god . . . what do I do?
               Father, where . . . my god . . . what?

OLD MAN Shush, son. Don't wake up
his pain. It makes him savage.
He looks dead, but he's alive.

HYLLOS This . . . alive?

OLD MAN Let the sleeper sleep.
Don't wake up his frenzies.
His infection is still roaring.

HYLLOS O no . . . the weight . . .   940
I'm the one who'll be mad!

HERAKLES *wakes, struggles to lift himself. He sees the statue*
of Zeus.

HERAKLES Zeus! God! What place is this? Where am I?
Who are these people watching
this endless torment? I'm destroyed, destroyed!
O the thing again, it's driving teeth in me!

OLD MAN I told you. Didn't I tell you to be quiet,
to let the sleep stay in his eyes?

HYLLOS Am I supposed to stand
and watch . . . this?

HERAKLES Kenaion . . . The altar! All my sacrifices!   950
Mine! And you, Zeus! This . . .
Is this the thanks you give me back?
This agony you've made of me, this outrage?

I wish these damned eyes had never seen you
and never had to see myself this way,
this incurable madness blossoming in me.

Can't somebody sing spells to me?
Lay your hands on? Heal this horror?

Do you need Zeus to say you can?
It would be a miracle to me. 960

The OLD MAN *tries to prop him up.*

Leave me alone! Let
me be! Let me die!
Alone!

Why are you touching me? Don't
touch me! You're killing me! Killing me!
You've woken up what was asleep!

It has me . . . Again. It's lunging through.
Where are the Greeks? Ungrateful!
I wore my useless life out
clearing monsters from your woods 970
and seas and where are you now? Somebody
put a sword in me! Set fire to me!

Tear the awful
head
from my abominable body!

OLD MAN You're his son, boy. Give me a hand. He's
too much for me. You're strong.
Your hands can help him more than mine.

HYLLOS I'm trying. My hands are trying.
But I can't make his life forget itself. 980
And neither can anyone. It's Zeus. He's doomed.

HERAKLES Son, where are you? Lift me.
Hold me . . . O god, what's happening to me?
The thing, again, again, it's pouncing,
lunging in me, leaping, destroying,
this unbelievable plague, this savage agony!

O goddess, Pallas, Sister, again, again!
Son, have pity on your father.
Take your knife. No one would blame you. Put it
in my chest. Heal the wild pain your damned mother   990
put there. O god, I'd give anything to see her suffer this,
the same destruction, this, she's given me.

Dear Death, you're God's brother. Do it!
End me! Let the pain sleep! Quick! Give me doom!

LEADER A great Lord
           to hear cry. What pain
               must have him! Huge!

HERAKLES It's torment even to speak of the sufferings
              these hands have labored through; the hot, awful loads
              on this back. But nothing Zeus' wife
              or that contemptible slavedriver, Eurystheus,
              ever made me do was anything to what the beautiful,   1000
              two-faced daughter of Oineus has woven me in,
              this net of Furies, this mutilation.
              It's nailed in me . . . It's eaten to inside me . . .
              It's moved in . . . Sucking my lungholes,
              all my good blood is swallowed. Its coils
              have wasted everything, my body, all my meat.
              No one, no hero I ever fought, not even the horde
              of giants born of the earth nor any monstrous,
              savage animal could do it . . . and no Greeks either,
              and not another place . . . Not anyone, from anywhere   1010
              I ever purified, could do what she, a weak,
              meaningless woman, without a sword, with nothing, by
                    herself,
              has done to me, defeated, conquered me, completely.
              Son, if you are my son and not your mother's boy,
              give me that woman, give me that dam of yours.
              Take your hands. Put her in my hands.
              I want to know which hurts you more . . . Me,
              like this, my agony, or her, when I make her suffer
              the punishment she deserves to suffer.

62

Go on, boy. Don't be a coward. Pity me.   1020
Anyone else would. Look at me,
moaning, bellowing like a wispy girl. Nobody
ever saw me like this before . . . never,
no matter where my damned luck took me.

Look! The hero!
All that time I was a woman!

Come here . . . closer . . . I'll show you your father.
I'll show you what's been done to me.
Look, under the cover, here . . . LOOK! ME! LOOK!
EVERYONE! . . . My muscles . . . ruined, pitiful . . .   1030
        Look again . . .
O DESTROYED!

Pain! Fire! The torment! Another time! Again,
wait, again, it's coming, I have to fight it,
that cruel, that eating in my sides, eating, eating . . .
O Lord down in the dark of Hell, take me now!
Give me fire, Zeus! Blast your bolts down! KING! KING!
Here, Father, my head, here. The thing's
consuming me, it's blossoming, festering . . .

O hands, my hands . . . Shoulders . . . Chest . . .
        My arms . . .
Is it still you? Did I really kill the man-eating lion   1040
in Nemea with you? No one else could come close,
no less strangle it. And the Hydra
from Lerna, you tamed that. And that din
of double-creatures, monstrosities, half-men, half-horse,
who spoke to no one and had no law but violence
and power? And the wild boar of Erymanthos
and the three-headed whelp of the Viper, horrible,
who lived under the earth, in Hell, unconquerable,
and the dragon guarding the golden fruit
at the end of the world, him too.   1050
And all the innumerable others.
These hands: no one ever triumphed over them.

And now I'm broken. Pieces. Waste.
And by what? I can't see it! It's invisible!
ME! Whose mother everyone says was the noblest of all.
ME! They said my father was Zeus himself, King of
      Heaven . . .

But let me tell you this: I might be nothing,
paralyzed in nothingness, but the one who did this
will know these hands, what they can do: give me her!
I have a message she can take back to the world: 1060
I punished evil when I was alive
and I punished it when I was dead.

LEADER O Greece! What will you do
      without this man . . .
         Mourn . . . Mourn . . .

HYLLOS Father, while you're quiet, let me speak.
      As sick as you are, I have to tell you something.
      Try to control your rage for a moment.
      Otherwise you'll never understand
      that vengeance wouldn't bring you joy,
      that your bitterness is useless.

HERAKLES If you have something to say, say it.   1070
      I'm in too much pain to have you riddling.

HYLLOS I want to tell you about my mother. What happened.
      The mistake she made. It was unintentional.

HERAKLES Damn you . . . You'd breathe her name to me?
      Your mother, who killed your father?

HYLLOS The way she is, she needs more than silence.

HERAKLES Oh, you're right. She does. She does.

HYLLOS And what she did today, that needs it, too.

64

HERAKLES Go ahead. But don't betray me.

HYLLOS She's dead. Just now. Slaughtered. 1080

HERAKLES Who killed her? What an awful miracle!

HYLLOS Nobody killed her. She did it herself.

HERAKLES O god, I wish I'd done that. She needed me for that!

HYLLOS If you knew the rest, you wouldn't rage this way.

HERAKLES A good start. Now, what are you saying?

HYLLOS This: she made a mistake. But she meant well.

HERAKLES Meant? Damn. Meant well, to kill your father?

HYLLOS She thought it was a love-charm she was sending.
       When she heard about your new marriage. That was the
              mistake.

HERAKLES Who could you get a drug that strong from here? 1090

HYLLOS It was Nessos, the centaur. In the old time.
       He told her it would make you want her.

HERAKLES THAT!
       THAT!
       THAT!
          The agony. I'm lost!
       Finished! FINISHED! My light—it's over now.
       I understand it now, my end; I'm there.

       Come here, Son. You have no father anymore.
       Go call your family. Call my mother,
       too: she slept with Zeus for nothing.

I want to give you all the oracles I know,
now, before I die.   1100

HYLLOS Alkmene isn't here, and neither are your children.
But there are enough of us
to do anything you could want. Just ask.

HERAKLES Then listen to what you have to do.
This is your chance to prove you're a man,
that you're the son of Herakles.
A long time ago, my father
prophesied that I wasn't going to die at the hands
of anything that breathed: something
would have to come from Hell to take me.   1110
And it's come true. I've been murdered by that brute
centaur: the dead kill the living, the holy promise.

Now listen again. In the mountains there are people
who still sleep on the ground, the Selloi.
They have an oak of my father's in their grove
and it speaks. No matter what your language is,
it speaks to you. It told me other things—
I even wrote them down—and they confirm the first.
This, now, the time we're living now,
is when I should have been released from labor.   1120
I thought it meant I'd prosper but it doesn't:
it means I die, that's all. The dead don't toil.

Son, look, it's
    revealed, look,
        everything, converging,
clear, brilliant,
    look, all of it, LOOK!
        LOOK!

I need your help now. Don't make me be angry
to convince you. Just say yes, and do it.

You ought to know at your age that obedience
to the father is the most important law.

HYLLOS Yes, father. I'm afraid of where you're taking us,
but yes, I'll do what you say.   1130

HERAKLES Then give me your hand. Your right hand.

HYLLOS An oath? Why?

HERAKLES Give it! Now! Mind me!

HYLLOS There , . . Here . . . Anything you want.

HERAKLES Swear. On the head of Zeus. Swear. My father's head.

HYLLOS Swear what? Tell me that at least.

HERAKLES To do the thing I ask.

HYLLOS I swear. I will. In the name of Zeus.

HERAKLES And pray to suffer if you violate it.

HYLLOS I won't suffer. I'll keep my word.   1140

HERAKLES Do you know the summit of Oita, Zeus' mountain?

HYLLOS Yes. I've sacrificed at the great altar.

HERAKLES You have to take me there.
Get all the friends you need
but I want you, your own hands, to carry me.
Then cut logs from the hardest oaks you can find
and tough, gnarled branches from olive trees.
Then put me on them. Then take a flaming torch
and set it on fire.
                    And no mourning,

no crying or carrying on. You're my son.   1150
And if you don't do it, all of it, you'll have my fury
and my curse, even from the next world, for all time.

HYLLOS What are you doing, Father? What are you asking me?

HERAKLES What has to be. And if you won't,
then get another father, I won't have you.

HYLLOS My god! Do you know what you're saying? .
I'd be your murderer! Your blood would be on me!

HERAKLES Not murderer . . . healer . . . doctor . . .
Only you can cure this evil.

HYLLOS I heal your flesh by burning it?   1160

HERAKLES If you're afraid of that, at least the rest.

HYLLOS I'll take you to Oita. I can do that much.

HERAKLES And make the pyre the way I told you?

HYLLOS Not with my own hands, but I'll have it done.
Everything else, yes. I won't stop you.

HERAKLES That's enough. More than enough.
Now one other little favor.

HYLLOS Of course. Anything you ask.

HERAKLES Do you know the girl . . . Eurytos' daughter?

HYLLOS Iole.   1170

HERAKLES Yes. This is what I want, Son:
after I'm dead, if you want to honor me
and honor your promises and not disobey,
then marry her. I don't want anyone else

68

being with her. She was mine, she slept with me.
I want you and her together, married. Say yes.
You've been obedient about so much that's important,
don't lose my good grace over something less.

HYLLOS You don't get angry with someone who's sick,
but how can I stand listening to him, to this? 1180

HERAKLES You won't do what I ask?

HYLLOS Who in the world . . . the woman whose fault it is
that my mother's dead and that you're *this* . . .
if someone wasn't swarming with avenging Furies,
would they choose her? Father, I'd be better off dead
with you than living with our bitterest enemy.

HERAKLES He won't carry out my dying wish, it seems.
You'll see:
the gods will curse your disobedience.

HYLLOS Tell me to do it now because you're sick. 1190

HERAKLES I am! You're stirring up my pain again!

HYLLOS What can I do? I'm trapped!

HERAKLES Why shouldn't you be? You don't honor your father!

HYLLOS Do I have to learn to do wrong, Father?

HERAKLES It isn't wrong. Not if it gives me joy.

HYLLOS Are you commanding it? Are you calling it right?

HERAKLES I command it. Before the gods, I'm commanding it.

HYLLOS Then I have to do it.
As long as the gods know it's your doing.
Who could call it wrong, obeying my father? 1200

69

HERAKLES   Finally. Good. No more words now.
            Just the favor. Get me on that fire.
            Don't let the pain bend me again.
            Quick. Lift me up. It's true. My labors are over.
            This is the end, the last and final end of Herakles.

HYLLOS   Nothing's preventing it, Father.
            You're commanding us. You're making us do it.

HERAKLES   Soul, be hard now! Don't let the sickness start you
            again. Put the steel bit in your teeth, weld it there,
            clamp your lips on it, stone against stone.   1210
            No tears.
            I want the finish of this welcome, unwelcome work
            to be joy.

            As HYLLOS *speaks, the* SERVANTS *lift the litter with* HERAKLES
                                                   and begin to exit.

HYLLOS   Lift him. Grant me forgiveness for what I'm doing.
            But the gods, let their ruthlessness in this,
            their cruelty, be remembered.
            They have their children, us. We call them Father.
            And they can bear to see such suffering.
            No one knows the future, but there is a present
            and the present is shame for them   1220
            and mourning for us, and for the victim, pain;
            solitude and pain.

            [To the LEADER OF THE CHORUS.]

            Girl, leave that house.
            You've seen dying, dreadful, and agony today
            and hideous suffering and nothing is here,
            nothing,
            none of all of it, that is not Zeus.

                    Exit HYLLOS, *following his father. Exit the* CHORUS.

            Night.

TRANSLATOR'S COMMENTS
NOTES
GLOSSARY

TRANSLATOR'S COMMENTS

The major difficulty in rendering the choruses is of course that they were originally set to music, sung, and danced, and that we have too little notion of what the music was to attempt to re-create it or "make it new." There are, then, two problems: how can the choruses achieve an integral, energetic role in the drama, given the fact that they must be simply spoken poetry and not music; and what is a valid approach to their performance?

I have tried to meet these problems first by trying to determine what the critical difference is between poetry and music. What is the irreducible element of each, irrespective of its elaboration in any particular work?

The basic unit of poetry is clearly the word. The basic unit of music might at first seem to be a sound, but this does not distinguish it from poetry since a word is itself a sound. So I would go further and say that music's basic element is repetition: the *repeated* sound. The repetition must occur in a pattern and this pattern can have a harmonic context, a rhythmic one: one of volume, duration, intensity, decay, etc.—or any or all of them. The human animal, given two sticks, will sooner or later produce at least a simple music. On the other hand, the most aesthetically complex culture will create a scale or scales, of however many modes, and a scale is at base a system of repetition. Once familiar with an individual mode, we need no more than a few notes of any phrase to predict without any intellection whatsoever what the resolution of the tonic—the unit of repetition—will be.

It would be beyond the scope of these remarks to inquire what exactly in the organism responds so precisely and dramatically to music. The pulse, the brain-patterns, the rhythms of life on the planet itself;

73

every possibility has been suggested. We can say with certainty though that the consciousness assumes an entirely unique kind of functioning while experiencing music: it seems to dissolve itself strangely into the body—we "hear" a drum or a cello, for instance, in our rib-cage—and music is simply not experienced at all unless there is this organic connection.

This is not true of poetry. It would be impossible to confuse the most lyrically complex poetry with the most resolutely simple song because this physical reaction is of an entirely different, more cerebrally determined order, and when we speak of the "music" of poetry, we do so only because there is no other word for what so profoundly happens to us as we experience it. The repetitive possibilities—sound, syllable, foot, phrase, line—for one thing cannot begin to approach those of music, but aside from this, poetry, and in particular tragedy as poetry, is in some sense the antithesis of music, the other limit of our range of responsiveness. We might go back and say that the basic unit of poetry is meaning: meaning experienced, struggled with, surrendered to; and tragedy is a continual spinning out of meaning and configurations of experience in a relentless, unresolving fugue of revelation; of the unknown and unknowable.

Perhaps we can further postulate that the function of the musical chorus in Greek tragedy, like that of comedy in Elizabethan, is to offer a chance for us to come to ourselves, as it were, to the other end, the source, the body, in order to gather the entire organism's resources to go on with this.

There is another factor, basic to any consideration of chorus. That it is, at least to a great extent, unison. It is, in its very substance, the audience, the community, experiencing itself, and this presents another problem in the presentation of chorus without music. Choral speaking, even at its very best, always has something about it of school children reciting. There is always an imperceptible pause while the group awaits one voice to lead it out of the silence, and any given sentence can actually have—from an orchestral point of view—an entirely different harmony, according to which voice had the courage to begin that particular sentence. What generally happens is that a kind of sing-song rhythm is generated—the same rhythm that children give to nursery rhymes, and adults to Bible-reading. I think this is because the human voice simply does not function in unison—in community—without music; perhaps for the fundamental reason that music is a simplification of time, an organization of the movement of our voices through time, and, without music, we founder.

In rendering the choruses of *Women of Trachis*, I have tried to take into account as many of these difficulties as possible. In trying to make at least a facsimile of the basic musical experience of the chorus, I have had to violate some of the precision of grammar and image that would normally be expected, and I have taken what might at first seem to be extraordinary liberties with the literal text by using many repetitions, generally of single words, but, occasionally, of phrases and whole line units. All these repetitions, however, I have taken from the variance of complex meanings which are carried by a word from one language to another. The texture I have tried to evoke obviously does not have as its "mode" any known musical structure. The resolution, to use musical terms, can happen within a few lines or a few words, in an obvious repetition, or it can extend over almost the length of the play, following the sub-pattern of repetition that Sophocles himself used (the word "shimmering" for instance).

The unison-speaking problem I have tried to resolve by substituting the control of sound through time with that of sound through space. There is, strictly speaking, no unison at all. Each single, descending line, as I have rendered it, represents an *individual* voice, coming from a spatially distinct point on the stage. By doing this, I have hoped the audience would experience the flow of lyric meaning both visually and aurally, and thus, by involving another sense as well as by breaking down the normal expectation of meaning-unit, a more organic—i.e. musical—reaction would be evoked.

The director obviously has a critical task in organizing the choruses spatially, and the speeches themselves will require greater skill from actors than ordinary choral "chant." Many of my notions here are, in fact, based on the exercise developed by Peter Brook to create a greater sense of dramatic community among his actors. A group of actors stands in a circle, one word of a Shakespearean line is given to each and then the group attempts to reproduce the line as it would be spoken by an individual. The results, Brook says, at first chaotic, are ultimately liberating for the actors and exhilarating for listeners. Some such exercise, possibly not quite as rigorous, would be needed here if the poetry is to cohere.

THE TRANSLATION

Statements of translating practices seem a particularly futile procedure. The translator may qualify, formulate or excuse, but the fact of the text speaks for itself; it is insolubly, or inconsolably, concrete.

TRANSLATOR'S COMMENTS

To readers who know the original language, a translation is an exercise in literary craftsmanship, and the attempt is defined from the beginning as one degree or another of failure. To those unfamiliar with the original, however, the search into the translation becomes a quest for the seed, the kernel, of sublimity and passion which presumably reside in the original, and a failure in this is of an entirely different order. It does not imply a mere rejection of the translator's effort, but a loss of the whole potential experience embodied in the work.

At the same time, a non-failure, a blossoming, however partial, of that kernel; a glimmer of the strength and relevance of the original, is a bringing forth of what previously was not. It is at this hopeful point that translation becomes in itself an art-form, and here a whole new area of difficulties is encountered: those of the given linguistic, poetic possibilities of the translator's own historical moment.

Lyrical range, philosophical urgency, intensity of expression, complexity of rhetoric, and metaphoric ingenuity: there is always, in any work, a balancing, one might almost say a bargaining, among all these, and their availability in a vital combination is determined more by the translator's cultural, literary milieu than by his own resources. The literatures we find compelling and significant always seem to us to delicately and judiciously fuse these elements. Other works, the ones to which we feel no affinity, never seem to. And of course our values, our needs, change relatively quickly and in a few years what was loved can seem stilted or opaque or simply exhausted, and what was previously brushed aside can suddenly illuminate.

In confronting such a cultural monument as one of Sophocles' tragedies, the translator becomes all too quickly aware of his own literary economics and its limitations; but at the same time there has to be a clearing away of some of the accumulations of reverence that confuse the work and the genius who made it. The translator begins to realize the compromises the poet Sophocles was constrained to make with *his* tradition and, perhaps more importantly, the compromises, often non-literary in origin, which were made *for* him.

Antonio Machado said: "Before writing a poem, one must imagine a poet capable of writing it." It is much the same with a translation. A Sophocles must be re-created who not only speaks in the language we do, but who in a sense lives in our own time with us, with our thoughts, culture, and tradition layered over his own. And this Sophocles must begin to make his choices over again. I suppose a sense of somewhat guilty presumption is inevitable.

This work was completed with the help of a grant from the Guggenheim Foundation.

76

I wish to thank Erving Goffman, Guy Davenport, Stephen Berg, Paul Zweig, and Lorand Gaspar, who all, at one time or another, offered ideas, criticism, tactics, and encouragement; William Arrowsmith, for whom the term "editor" does not begin to capture the degree of his labor and the quality of his involvement, and Catherine Mauger, for everything.

C.K.W.

NOTES ON THE TEXT

1 *The palace of Keyx* . . . The manuscripts of Greek tragedy contain no stage directions. We have been sparing in-our reconstruction. In the original production all performers were male and masked. Since the Greek tragedians were allotted, in addition to a chorus,.only three actors for the performance of all speaking parts, it is probable that both Deianeira and Herakles were played by the most accomplished of the three, the protagonist appointed by the state. It is impossible to assess what effect, if any, this conventional doubling of roles, so intriguing in terms of twentieth-century psychology, exercised upon an ancient audience.

10 Achelöos   Herakles' combat with this creature was a popular subject in ancient literature and art. In order to magnify the importance of Deianeira in the episode Sophocles omits reference to what seems to have been its traditional center of interest—the Horn of Amalthaia, a magic cornucopia, which Herakles carried away as his principal prize of victory.

14 *shimmering*   The first occurrence of *aiolos*, one of the play's key words. The adjective appears thrice hereafter (94; 132; 818) and is found only twice elsewhere in all Sophocles' preserved work. The Greek word evokes a complexity of associations, but primarily a sense of swift mutability, sometimes from inertia to motion, sometimes from darkness to light. When applied to human fortune and human behavior, however, it has particularly unsettling implications of impermanence, unreliability, and deception. Thus Aeschylus refers to the ·"mutable misfortunes of men" (*ta aiol' anthrōpōn kaka*: *Suppliants* 328), Solon to the "shifty speech of tyrants" (*epos aiolon*: Fragment 10.7), and Pindar to Odysseus' capacity for the "shifty lie" (*aiolon pseudos*: *Nemean* 8.25). For additional comment, cf. the Introduction, I.

41 *He killed poor Iphitos* Cf. the Introduction, IV, and the note on 244-323.

42-3 *people / we hardly know* By this vague reference to anonymous hosts Sophocles glancingly nods at the tradition which set the scene of this story
at the palace of Keyx, king of Trachis. Elsewhere he ignores the dramatically inconvenient fact that Herakles and Deianeira are merely
guests at the house where the action centers. All that follows creates
and sustains the illusion that the palace and the loyalties of the local
Chorus belong solely to the hero and his wife.

56 *so many children* Extant ancient tradition records four offspring of the Her-
akles-Deianeira marriage in addition to Hyllos. Only here and in a
passing reference at the end of the play (1101) does Sophocles acknowledge the existence of these siblings. The pre-eminence given
throughout the play to Hyllos' filial role is crucial to some of the
tragedy's most powerful effects, isolating the son in his suffering and
preparing for the suggestive father-son parallelism noted in the Introduction, V.

61f *Enter Hyllos, returning, . . . running* It is puzzling that Sophocles fails to
provide Hyllos' running entrance with the explicit motivation com-
monly found in the other plays. The suggestion has been made that he
rushes in to report fresh news about Herakles' Oichalian campaign.
This seems unlikely; for neither does Hyllos behave like other Sophoclean "messengers," nor is he treated as one by the other characters
on stage. More probably the vigorous mode of his entrance is intended to strike an effective contrast with the remarkably static pose
struck by the passive Deianeira. Our stage direction is intended only
to emphasize the necessity for a director to give some visible logic to
an entrance which otherwise might strike an audience as somewhat
absurd. Some such measure was surely taken by Sophocles in the
original production.

71 *a woman . . . he ploughed* Lichas later (244ff) identifies this woman as
Omphale; cf. the note on those lines. In the context of Deianeira's
recent Herakles-farmer simile (34ff), this reference to "ploughing"
(literally: "he has been toiling . . . throughout the past ploughing
season") suggests a touch of Sophoclean irony. Deianeira will soon
discover that her farmer-husband has indeed been laboring in another
woman's "field." The Chorus later reveals (810) that Zeus' oracle
also measured the hero's destiny by "ploughing-times." For the same
metaphor, common in Greek, cf. *Oedipus* 1497.

100 *the sea-pit*   Probably the straits separating Greece from Asia Minor.

101 *the doubled continents*   Precisely what vista the poet intends to evoke remains
unclear. A reference to Europe and Asia is usually assumed. Others
have seen an allusion to the Pillars of Herakles, which mark the Med-
iterranean's western outlet between Africa and Spain. This gives a
more impressive sweep to the Chorus' vision.

105 *like the blinded bird*   This may be intended to suggest no more than the picture of a bird lamenting the loss of nestlings, one of the commonplace sorrow-images of Greek tragedy. There may, however, also be a
hint of the nightingale's eternal sorrow, a theme which, though no
less shopworn, is particularly appropriate to Deianeira's case. Greek
myth identified the nightingale with Prokne, who was driven by the
discovery of her husband's infidelity to destroy her son, thereby con-
demning herself to ceaseless lamentation.

116 *seed of Kadmos*   Geographically but not genetically accurate. Herakles was
born at Thebes, of which Kadmos was the founder and first ruler,
but he possessed no blood connection with the Kadmean line.

156 *covenants*   A radical departure from the traditional interpretation of the word
which Sophocles has written here. That word, *ksunthēmata*, literally
denotes objects of mutual agreement. The prevailing view is that the
reference here is to the conventional symbols of writing, i.e. the
letters of the alphabet. This specific usage, however, is unparalleled
elsewhere in Greek literature. Nor does the occasional application
of the word to "codes" and "passwords" point in that direction; for
such agreements imply elements of personal involvement and con-
scious consent, whereas the alphabet is merely a convention to which
one is born, automatically accepted without any sense of voluntarily
entering into an act of accord with all men of letters. We cannot,
therefore, believe that Sophocles intended to write anything as otiose
as "a tablet inscribed with the letters of the alphabet." A more reliable
guide to his meaning is his own use of the word to denote com-
pacts of a personal nature at the only two places where it appears elsewhere in his work. Both belong to *Oedipus at Kolonos*, where men-
tion is made of a mysterious covenant between the hero and God
(46) and of an agreement struck between Theseus and Perithöos in
preparation for their descent to the Underworld (1594). For the implications of Sophocles' use of the word in Deianeira's speech, cf.
the Introduction, V.

168-9 *sacred oak* / . . . *dove-priestesses* This venerable oracular shrine was originally consecrated to Zeus. By Sophocles' time Dione, an earth-mother
figure, and Aphrodite, Zeus' daughter by Dione, were also worshipped
there. Consultants of the oracle were brought before Zeus' sacred oak.
Local priestesses divined the sense of the god's response from the
movements of its leaves and branches and articulated the message
for visitors. Why these priestesses were called "doves" is not clear,
though it is probable that the term was to some extent connected
with the prominence of doves in Aphrodite's cult.

174-5 *Wait . . . joy* Throughout the translation, lines belonging to the Leader
of the Chorus have been subdivided into three descending units in
order to maintain conformity with the typography of the passages
spoken by the Chorus as a whole. In the case of the Leader's lines,
however, this triadic arrangement is intended to imply neither the
presence of lyrics in the original nor the necessity for each descending
unit to be spoken by a different voice. In the Greek the Leader, except for one brief lapse into lyrics (see the note on 855-6), expresses
herself in the regular iambic rhythms of spoken dialogue.

175 *a wreath* It seems to have been the custom for Greek messengers to wear garlands when bearing good news. Kreon, arriving from Delphi at the
beginning of *Oedipus*, also wears a wreath.

196 *Oita* This is the first of four mentions of the mountain famous as the site of
Herakles' self-immolation and apotheosis; cf. 425, 618, 1141. For the
importance of these references to the creation of false expectation in
the audience, cf. the Introduction, V.

210 *double-struck* Literally: "double-fired"; she carries torches in both hands.

211 *neighbor bride-nymphs* In Greek the same word (*numphos*) serves to denote
both "nymph" and "bride." Both senses have been asserted in the
translation in order to preserve the ironic ambiguity of the original.
The Chorus invokes the Nymphs of the Trachinian neighborhood;
immediately a "bride" appears close at hand. It is Iole.

222 *look-out . . . march* Deianeira's use of military metaphor is another twist of
Sophoclean irony. She will soon discover that Iole's arrival does in fact
constitute a dangerous invasion. The metaphor of the "march" is repeated in the last line of this scene. (480)

244-323 *It wasn't only that . . . / . . . when you want to* It is impossible to communicate to a modern audience the interplay of tensions with which Sophocles has charged this scene of deception. The Greek spectators, despite the poet's uncharacteristic failure to forewarn them of the herald's deceitful intent, were instantly alerted to his duplicity by their own familiarity with the traditional outlines of the story. They must have guessed at once the identity of the bedraggled princess whose absence from Lichas' narrative is no less conspicuous than her presence in the theater; and they must have clearly discerned the half-truths with which he tries to spare Deianeira's feelings and save his master's reputation. According to what seems to have been the orthodox version of the story, Iphitos was murdered not while searching for innocent strays (267) but while seeking to recover horses stolen from Oichalia—some said by Herakles himself in spite at Eurytos' refusal to surrender Iole. Similarly, the original audience must have sensed in Lichas' reference to the archery contest (259) the same oddity which compelled an ancient commentator on this passage to remark: " This is a peculiar version; for he (Eurytos) not only boasted about his children but also set Iole as a prize for archery and then failed to hand her over when Herakles was victorious." In the original, several passages of unusually stilted Greek in Lichas' long speech seem designed to reflect the embarrassment of an inexperienced and reluctant liar.

246-7 *a bought slave . . . / . . . God's work* Herakles' sale to Omphale was imposed by Apollo, at Zeus' request, to purify the pollution incurred by Iphitos' murder and to provide blood-money to the victim's relatives.

261 *magical arrows* Herakles possessed, as a gift from Apollo, a miraculous bow with infallible arrows. At his death the hero bequeathed these to Philoktetes, the kindler of his pyre, in whose hands they ultimately proved instrumental to the Greek victory at Troy.

262-5 *called him a slave . . . / . . . when he was drunk* There is no trace of these insults elsewhere in ancient tradition. They are meant by Sophocles to be recognized for what they are: something freely invented by Lichas to conceal the true motive behind Herakles' destruction of Oichalia.

273-4 *It wasn't the killing, / but the guile* A valiant attempt by Lichas to mitigate the seriousness of his master's crime. The original audience, familiar

with Zeus' important role as guarantor of their venerable laws of
hospitality, must have immediately sensed the special pleading. Far
more outrageous than the stealthy execution of the murder was the
hero's choice of victim: a helpless guest.

324-421 *Wait!* . . . / . . . *passion for the girl.*   There are clear hints of malicious
pleasure in the bluntness with which the Messenger breaks the truth
to Deianeira and cross-examines the embarrassed Lichas. The motivation for this spite—and for his refusal to quit the stage after perform-
ing his function as self-appointed messenger—has been left implicit
in the action: he is frustrated by Deianeira's failure to respond to his
pointed request for a reward (187f) and chagrined at having his
thunder stolen by the arrival of Herakles' herald. In his fondness for
legal jargon and in his relish at assuming a prosecutorial role he has
much in common with the victims of Athenian jury-mania satirized
by Aristophanes in his *Wasps*. Of all Sophocles' anonymous minor
characters, including the candid Watchman in *Antigone*, the Messenger is the most carefully and the most colorfully sketched.

395-8 *Just* . . . *just-ice* . . . *unjust* . . . *Injustice*   The Messenger, in his foren-
sic fervor, attempts to dazzle Lichas with malicious play upon *dikē*,
the Greek word for punishment and justice.

416 *to marry*   Literally: "as a wife (*damar*) for Herakles." Sophocles stresses that
the hero intends Iole to play a permanent and prestigious role within
his house. The Greek word *damar* always denotes legitimate wife,
never concubine or mistress. It is unclear whether or not the audience
is meant to assume that Herakles intends to divorce Deianeira. Deianeira obviously does not think so (cf. 521ff), but this may be intended
to reflect a natural reluctance to face painful facts. The critical point
established by the Messenger here is that Iole represents something
far more dangerous than a philandering husband's passing fancy. It
makes little difference whether Deianeira is confronted by divorce or
by some intolerable form of bigamy. What matters is the unprece-
dented threat to the security of her cherished role as the only true
"wife" of Herakles.

446 *more women than I can count*   According to Greek tradition Herakles sired
sons by some sixty different women, including Omphale. In equating
his interest in Iole with these previous fleeting affairs Deianeira seems
not yet to have grasped the key point stressed by the Messenger at
416; cf. the preceding note.

481 *Love's goddess* Aphrodite.

484-8 *Zeus . . . was taken in . . . and Death . . . and even the whole earth*
Sophocles emphasizes two aspects of Love's dominion: its cosmic
reach and its powers of deception. The first is implicit in its victories
over Zeus (sky), Death (Underworld), and Poseidon (earth and sea);
the second is explicitly affirmed as a hint of Deianeira's imminent resort to guile.

501 *her choosing wand* The effect of Sophocles' text is enriched by an untranslatable ambiguity between images of Love, wielder of the athletic
umpire's staff, and Love, wielder of the sorceress' wand. Both are
denoted by the word used here: *rhabdos*. The athletic image is
charged with irony. Aphrodite stands serenely refereeing a contest in
which no holds are barred.

512 *and I can see it . . . could tell* In the Greek the Chorus seems to say: "I am
a mother in the sort of things I speak." All attempts to prove that
some sense can be extracted from this inanity have failed. Faced by
such incurable corruption in the text, we have found free invention
the only recourse.

522-4 *a slut . . . / . . . under the same blanket* Deianeira's sudden lapse into
uncharacteristically coarse language is clearly intended to reveal the
anger now rising to challenge her high principles of conjugal toler-
ance. This whole speech is remarkable for the subtlety with which it
illuminates Deianeira's inner struggle to stifle unfamiliar and fright-
ening forces of resentment.

548-9 *carrying me like that / . . . he put his hands on me* Sophocles pictures
Nessos carrying Deianeira "on his shoulders." We have eliminated
this detail, finding it an unlikely posture for the putting on of hands.
Sophocles makes Nessos' attack on Deianeira, like Herakles' on Iole,
an unprovoked assault. There is some indication that in the traditional version of the story it was presented as revenge for a wound
inflicted by the hero during the course of his battle with the centaurs.
Cf. the note on 1044.

580 *No matter how shameful* Deianeira's sense of shame derives partly from the
deceit to which she has been driven and partly from her resort to
lover's magic, something the Greeks considered both dangerous and
disreputable.

597 *like a newborn child*   Again the Greek possesses untranslatable ambiguity. Deianeira has vowed that she will make Herakles a "new sacrificer in a new robe." For the Greeks "newness" had a double aspect. To the extent that it suggested freshness and ingenuity it was a quality to be desired; to the extent that it suggested the strange and unexpected it was considered distinctly ominous. Here Deianeira intends the first sense; but the original audience, already aware of the outcome, was intended to sense the ironic aptness of the second: Herakles will indeed soon become a "novel" sacrificer in a "novel" robe. Finding it impossible to reproduce this effect in English, the translator has substituted for sinister "newness" the vulnerability of the newborn.

605 *to fall on my face*   Lichas uses a common Greek expression for failure: "I shall not be tripped up." By the choice of metaphor Sophocles ironically prefigures the moment when Herakles grasps the herald by the ankle and hurls him to his death; cf. 762ff. In the original, Lichas prefaces this assurance with the condition: "If I hold firm command of Hermes' escort-craft." There is an additional irony here deriving from Hermes' double function as both patron god of heralds and escort of souls to the Underworld. We have omitted the reference since its point would be lost on a modern audience.

616-22 *the harbor . . . where the gates are*   The geographical features enumerated by the Chorus all belong to the local landscape: the hot springs from which Thermopylai (hot-gates) gained its name; the Malian Gulf; the eastern shore of central Greece; and Anthela, where the Amphictyonic Council met to administer the affairs of Apollo's shrine at Delphi.

620 *the Huntress-Goddess*   Artemis, who seems to have been considered the protectress of this segment of the Greek coast.

631 *twelve months*   There is an apparent discrepancy between this description of the duration of Herakles' absence and the critical period of fifteen months twice stressed previously by Deianeira (46f; 163f). Those who have attempted to explain away this inconsistency have argued either that the poet forgets what he has said in the earlier scenes, or that the reference is limited to the period of servitude in Lydia, or that it denotes the last of the twelve years which the Chorus first mentions nearly two hundred lines later (809). Few readers will find much consolation in such improbable answers to this perplexing question. Regrettably, a more satisfying alternative has yet to be suggested.

636-7 *the stung-mad / war-god*   Ares. The Greek suggests a latent image of a bull, goaded to madness by the gadfly's sting. The passage thus provides a prophetic glimpse of Herakles bellowing under the sting of Nessos' poison; cf. 790, 1022.

644 *soothed*   Again Sophocles' language is charged with untranslatable ambiguity. The play is upon the Greek verb khriō, which, though usually used to denote the "smearing" of soothing ointments, is employed four times in Aeschylus' *Prometheus* to describe the maddening sting of the gadfly. It is the former sense which dominates here and in Deianeira's long speech at the beginning of the next scene, where this verb and its cognates are four times repeated. Its last recurrence is in the next stasimon, where Hyllos' disclosure prompts the Chorus to assert the secondary sense in their description of the "stinging" venom of the Hydra, cf. 819.

658 *sheep's wool*   Raw wool was prescribed by a variety of ancient rituals, including lovers' magic and sacrifice to the spirits of the dead. It is thus doubly appropriate for Deianeira's rite. She thinks she is binding Herakles' affections; in reality she is sacrificing him to the shade of his enemy, Nessos.

666 *like a law on a bronze tablet*   By this simile Sophocles ironically recalls the tablet on which Herakles' oracles are inscribed; cf. 50, 156. The play's final scene reveals that Nessos' instructions do, in fact, reflect Zeus' ineradicable writing of the hero's destiny.

686 *the way the earth on a grave boils*   Our own addition, designed to clarify the suggestions of chthonic ritual implicit in the Greek: "as when the rich juice of the blue harvest from Bacchos' vine is poured out on the ground." The pouring of wine upon the ground is a conspicuous feature of Greek offerings to the dead. The suggestion of such ritual is particularly appropriate at the moment of Deianeira's discovery that she has sacrificed her husband to his dead enemy. Cf. the note on 658.

699-700 *even hurt Cheiron, and Cheiron was a god*   During the aftermath of their battle with Herakles (cf. the note on 1044) some of the centaurs fled to Cheiron for protection. One of the poisoned arrows launched by the hero in his pursuit passed through its intended target and struck his innocent friend. As the immortal victim of immortal venom, Cheiron would have been condemned to eternal agony had not the mortal Prometheus agreed to exchange lots with him, thereby enabling the centaur to suffer a merciful death.

780 *his eyes were rolling* For the Greeks rolling eyes were characteristic of both madmen and raging bulls. The latent animal image is consistent with Sophocles' emphasis on Herakles' bestialization throughout the play and is reinforced by the hero's "bellowing" a few lines below (790).

783 *Even if you have to die* Herakles' readiness to destroy his son stands in striking contrast with Deianeira's recently announced readiness to destroy herself as proof of her devotion.

798-804 *crawl . . . crawl . . . crawl . . . crawl* Hyllos, who has already—with unwitting accuracy—compared Deianeira's gift to the "venom from a snake" (754), finds an unexpected aptness in the verb innocently introduced by the Chorus and bitterly exploits its suggestion of reptilian movement by emphatic repetition. Though the verb in question (*herpō*) had already by Sophocles' time come into somewhat indiscriminate use for motion of all kinds, it is here intended to be felt in its original sense. One of the forms used by Hyllos (*herpetō*) strongly suggests the Greek word for reptile (*herpeton*—"crawling thing").

809 *the twelve years* The play's first indication that Zeus' oracle specified twelve years as the period of Herakles' appointed toil. Few readers, we suspect, will share the distress felt by some critics at the Chorus' sudden revelation of a fact which, according to the strict logic of dramatic premise, they have no right to know. That the sudden clarification of the meaning of the oracle is accompanied by a sudden clarification of its terms possesses a poetic logic of its own. For the ironic point of the reference to "ploughing-times" (810), see the note on 71.

843 *the servant, Love, the silent* In this climactic image Aphrodite, whose sovereignty over the action has remained unchallenged since its affirmation by the Chorus in the first stasimon, stands finally revealed as no more than the instrument of a higher power still—the will of Zeus. The impact of the passage is intensified by an ironic reminiscence of the two conspicuously "silent" women—first Iole and most recently Deianeira—whom Aphrodite herself has employed to serve Zeus' purpose.

855-6 *Deianeira has disappeared . . . without a single step* The rather contrived
formality of this remark suggests that the Nurse enters relatively composed and eager to deliver an impressive narrative of what has happened inside. During the exchange which follows (857-75) she becomes flustered by the Chorus Leader's increasingly impatient
interruptions. In the original the aura of confusion is intensified by a
break into irregular lyric metres (863-75) and by repeated shifts of
speaker within the line.

884-5 *bellowing / that she was alone* A clear echo of the first stasimon's climactic
image of Deianeira, the lost and lonely calf; cf. 516.

918-21 *Anyone who tries . . . is suffered through* These lines bear a striking re-
semblance to the commonplace expressions of resignation with which
choruses frequently conclude Greek tragedies. By this suggestion of
finality Sophocles brings into the highest possible relief the sharp line
of demarcation between the play's two constituent tragedies and their
isolated protagonists.

921ff *Enter Hyllos . . . exit* Hyllos' movements at this point raise a difficult
problem. There is no indication in the text that he appears at any
time during the interval between his exit into the palace after 805
and the beginning of his exchange with the Old Man at 930. On the
other hand, the text clearly suggests that in the finale he enters not
from the palace but in the same party with Herakles and his attend-
ants. If the action is to be intelligible, the route of Hyllos' return to
Herakles with the litter which he has prepared inside "to bring his
father in" (882) must somehow be clarified for the audience. Since
the presumption of an invisible "backdoor" is alien to the conventions
of Greek tragedy, we can only conclude that Sophocles caused Hyllos
to enter and exit, in silence and without comment from those on
stage, here at the end of the Nurse's speech and before the beginning
of the final stasimon. Though this procedure is itself unparalleled elsewhere in Greek tragedy, it seems clearly preferable to the only alternative which has yet been suggested: Hyllos enters *from the palace* after
926 and finds his intention to return to Herakles anticipated by his
father's arrival. If Sophocles intended the hero to arrive without any
assistance from Hyllos he would hardly have created superfluous difficulties by stressing the son's preoccupation with the bed.

927 *like a nightbird* Cf. the note on 105.

930-94 *O my god . . . / . . . Give me doom!* No translation can hope to do more than hint at the impact of this passage in its original production. Here Sophocles uses every available resource—spectacle, flute, and song—to raise his audience's emotions to an excruciatingly high pitch. During their approach to the palace the hero and his party chant in anapestic measures, a conventional marching rhythm (930-60). At 961 the attempt to move Herakles causes him to erupt in agonized song. Then the Old Man and Hyllos, succumbing to the lyric intensity of this outburst, themselves begin to sing (976-81). Not until the Chorus re-establishes the regular iambic rhythms of dialogue at 995 does this frenzied music die. The unsettling effect of the whole lyric exchange (961-94) is reinforced by a striking asymmetry of metrical structure and by an ironic exploitation of the dactylic hexameter, the rhythm of Greek epic, to underline the magnitude of Herakles' loss of heroic grandeur.

956 *blossoming* Many readers may be surprised to learn that Sophocles has appropriated this striking metaphor from the technical terminology of Greek medicine, where "blossom" (*anthos*) denotes a pustulant efflorescence. He repeats the effect at 1038. Since the metaphor is not likely to have died by Sophocles' time and since it may well be intended to echo ironically Deianeira's image of Herakles plucking Iole's youthful "blossom" (*anthos*: 532), the literal force of the word has been stressed throughout the translation.

987 *Pallas, Sister* The goddess Athena, herself a child of Zeus. We have added "Sister" to stress the special intimacy of her relationship with the hero. In Greek myth she serves not only as his half-sister but also as his protectress, assisting him at various points in his career and ultimately aiding in his apotheosis by escorting him from Mt. Oita to Olympos.

993 *Death . . . God's brother* Another relative. As Zeus' brother, Death (Hades) is also Herakles' uncle.

998 *Zeus' wife* Hera, whose persecution of her husband's bastard son is notorious in Greek myth. It is she who sends serpents to destroy the infant Herakles in his cradle and who later drives the hero to murder, in a fit of madness, his children by the Theban princess Megara. Sophocles' allusion to Hera's malice is intentionally vague. His dramatic premise precludes any specific reference to the hero's previous marriage and its tragic outcome.

1008 *giants born of the earth* These giants were spawned by Gē (Earth) and
Ouranos (Sky) to attack Zeus and the other children of Kronos after
they had usurped their father's throne and defeated his allies, the
Titans, in battle. Warned by an oracle that the giants could only be
destroyed by a mortal, Zeus enlisted the aid of Herakles, who subsequently destroyed them with his arrows.

1029 *under the cover* Most probably the lion-skin which, though not anywhere
mentioned in the text, serves everywhere in ancient art as one of the
hero's indispensable identification marks. As such, it must have been
made visible in the original staging of the scene.

1040-41 *lion / in Nemea* The destruction of this beast was the first of the labors
imposed upon Herakles by Eurystheus. After throttling it with his
bare hands, the hero carried the carcass back to the king's palace. Eurystheus was supposed to have been so terrified by the sight of the
creature that he ordered Herakles in the future to deposit his victims
outside the city gates. The lion's hide became a conventional feature
of the hero's costume; cf. the note on 1029.

1044 *monstrosities, half-men, half-horse* The centaurs, who attacked Herakles in
rage at his having sampled a special wine reserved solely for their own
enjoyment. It was during the aftermath of this battle that the hero ac-
cidentally wounded Cheiron; cf. the note on 699-700.

1046 *wild boar of Erymanthos* The destruction of this creature, another bane to
the inhabitants of southern Greece, also belongs to the hero's labors
for Eurystheus.

1047 *three-headed whelp of the* Viper Kerberos, watchdog of Hades' gates. He was
thought to possess, in addition to a forbidding multiplicity of heads,
a mane of snakes and a dragon's tail. At Eurystheus' command Herakles descended to Hades, overpowered this creature without aid of
weapons, and brought it back alive to the world above. Kerberos'
mother, Echidna (Viper), was another monster, half-woman, half-
snake. According to some ancient authors, the journey which brought
Herakles to the palace of Oineus was prompted by an encounter with
the shade of Meleager, Deianeira's brother, during this visit to the
Underworld.

1049 *the dragon guarding the golden fruit* Herakles was ordered by Eurystheus to
bring back the golden apples presented by Earth to Hera as a wed-

ding gift and entrusted to the Hesperides, daughters of Night, for safe-keeping. As a deterrent to thieves, Hera stationed a hundred-headed dragon to guard the miraculous fruit. Sophocles follows the tradition in which Herakles himself destroys this monster and makes away with the apples. According to an alternative version, the hero persuaded Atlas to steal the fruit.

1113-14 *people / who . . . the Selloi* The local tribe which administered Zeus' sanctuary at Dodona. Homer, at *Iliad* XVI. 235, notes that in addition to dispensing with beds they failed to wash their feet. It is not clear whether these peculiar habits were noted as evidence of ascetic principle or as proof of barbarian origin.

1115-16 *an oak . . . / and it speaks* Cf. the note on 168-9.

1121 *I thought it meant I'd prosper* In view of Deianeira's vivid description of the gloomy mood in which Herakles left Trachis (154ff), the reference must be to recent confidence instilled by the release from Omphale and the victory at Oichalia.

1146-7 *from the hardest oaks . . . / . . . from olive trees* Literally: "from the deep-rooted oak and the virile wild olive." The striking specificity of these instructions casts an aura of sacrificial ritual over the hero's sudden resolve to destroy himself by fire; cf. the Introduction, V. The two components of the pyre aptly represent the two partners in the compact which has produced it. Zeus' sacred oak has foretold the hero's destiny, and the wild olive was thought to have been brought to Greece by Herakles to provide shade and victors' wreaths for his father's festival at Olympia; cf. Pindar, *Olympian* III. 13ff and Pausanias V.7.7.

1161 *at least the rest* Hyllos must be excused from the actual kindling of the pyre since Greek tradition reserves this service for Philoktetes (or his father). As the favor by which Philoktetes won the legacy of Herakles' miraculous bow, this detail of the myth was too important to ignore; cf. the note on 261.

1167 *Now one other little favor* We remain unpersuaded by those critics who have attempted to deny the callousness of this casual addendum. The argument that Herakles' arrangement of a marriage for his captive is intended as proof of his capacity for compassion is patently inconsistent with Sophocles' emphasis on the hero's pitiless response to the pain which this "little favor" inflicts upon his son. Another view assumes that Sophocles felt compelled by audience expectation to account for the existence of this intrinsically improbable marriage in established Greek tradition. We find this inconceivable. At this overpowering moment no audience could be expected to be preoccupied with reflections upon mythical genealogies. The Hyllos-Iole marriage would never have come to mind had not the poet chosen to make an issue of it. For our view of the significance of this choice, cf. the Introduction, V.

1208 *Soul, be hard now* Here the Greek text shifts from the iambic trimeters of spoken dialogue to chanted anapests. The change marks the beginning of the processional exit which closes the play.

1209-10 *steel bit . . . / . . . stone against stone* An intentionally free rendering of Sophocles' perplexing phrase: "a stone-glued bit of steel." Herakles seems to picture himself as a marble horse to which, in accordance with a common practice of Greek sculptors, metal harness has been welded with lead. The image is particularly suited to this context where the hardening and the taming of the hero's spirit are simultaneously affirmed. Others have assumed a reference to a particularly painful type of bit studded with sharp stones. This attractive suggestion is unfortunately unsupported by any evidence that stone-studded bits ever existed in Greece.

1223-7 *Girl . . . Zeus* The manuscripts reflect great confusion as to whether these lines belong to Hyllos or the Leader of the Chorus. We unhesitatingly assign them to Hyllos. Their tone is consistent with the bitterness of his preceding remarks (1215-22), and they are readily intelligible as an instruction to the Leader to initiate the exit of the Chorus. Those who have supported the attribution to the Leader have been driven to a desperate search for a "girl" for her to address. Some have found her in Iole, assuming her presence in the scene despite Sophocles' failure to indicate this seemingly pointless reappearance at any point in the preceding dialogue. Others argue that the Leader uses the singular "girl" to address her fourteen fellow chorus members, an improbable procedure unparalleled elsewhere in Sophoclean tragedy. Such are the drastic measures required if the conclusion of the play is to be restored to orthodox form by providing a conventional closing remark from the Chorus. They reflect, in our view, a perverse reluctance to accept the obvious: that in omitting a choral tag Sophocles deliberately defies convention in order to sustain the agonizingly inconclusive effect which he has contrived for this finale.

I am grateful to the President, Directors, and Trustees of Bryn Mawr College for their generous award of the year's leave of absence during which this collaboration has been completed. To Richmond Lattimore and Richard Hamilton, colleagues past and present, and to William Arrowsmith, the editor of this series, I give special thanks for their scrutiny of the manuscript of the Introduction and Notes. My debt to their perceptive criticisms and suggestions is enormous. The responsibility for whatever errors, idiocies, or imperfections still remain is solely mine.

· G.W.D.

GLOSSARY

ACHELÖOS, monstrous spirit of the major Aitolian river which bears
the same name.

ALKMENE, wife of the Argive exile Amphitryon, in whose guise Zeus
visited her to sire Herakles.

APOLLO, god of prophecy, healing, and lyric poetry; brother of Artemis.

ARTEMIS, virgin goddess of the hunt, protectress of the small and helpless; sister of Apollo.

CENTAUR, a common monster-type characterized by the fusion of
human head and torso with the four legs and body of a horse;
notorious for its lust.

CHEIRON, an atypically humane and civilized centaur; immortal son of
Kronos and mentor and friend to many Greek heroes; acciden-
tally wounded and eventually destroyed by one of Herakles'
poisoned arrows.

DEIANEIRA, daughter of Oineus, wife of Herakles, and mother of
Hyllos.

DODONA, a town in the wilds of northwestern Greece; cult-place of
Zeus and site of his sacred oak, the oldest of all Greek oracles.

ERYMANTHOS, a mountain in southern Greece; haunt of the savage
boar destroyed by Herakles during his labors for Eurystheus.

EUBOIA, the large island lying just off the eastern shore of central
Greece; adjacent at its upper extremity to the territory of
Trachis and at its lower to the shores of Attika; site, at the
north, of Cape Kenaion; at the south, of Oichalia.

EURYSTHEUS, Argive king, notorious as the cruel taskmaster for whom
Herakles was compelled, by divine decree, to labor for twelve
years.

EURYTOS, king of Oichalia, father of Iphitos and Iole.

FURIES, subterranean spirits of darkness dedicated to the pursuit and punishment of murderers.

HERAKLES, son of Zeus and Alkmene; the hero of the famous Labors.

HYDRA, a gigantic, many-headed serpent; constant plague to the inhabitants of Lerna until destroyed by Herakles at Eurystheus' command; source of the venom with which the hero tipped his infallible arrows.

HYLLOS, son of Herakles and Deianeira.

IPHITOS, son of Eurytos and brother of Iole; treacherously murdered, while a guest at Tiryns, by Herakles.

KADMOS, founder and first king of Thebes.

KENAION, a small promontory at the northwest tip of Euboia; site of Herakles' triumphal sacrifice to Zeus.

KRONOS, son of the primitive sky-god Ouranos and father of Zeus, who subsequently overthrew him to become the supreme Greek deity.

LERNA, a coastal region of southern Greece just south of Argos; home of the Hydra destroyed by Herakles.

LICHAS, Herakles' herald; deliverer of Iole to Deianeira and of the fatal robe to Herakles; ultimately murdered by the hero as punishment for his unwitting participation in Deianeira's scheme.

LOKRIS, the coastal region lying immediately to the southeast of Trachis and facing Cape Kenaion.

LYDIA, a barbarian realm in Asia Minor ruled by Queen Omphale.

NEMEA, a valley in southern Greece, approximately midway between Corinth and Mycenae; home of the monstrous lion destroyed by Herakles as his first labor for Eurystheus; later the site of an important sanctuary of Zeus and the festival of the Nemean Games.

NESSOS, a centaur killed by Herakles in reprisal for an attack upon Deianeira; donor of the charm which finally destroys the hero.

OICHALIA, a city on Euboia; home of Eurytos, Iphitos, and Iole; attacked and destroyed by Herakles.

OINEUS, Aitolian king and Deianeira's father.

OITA, a mountain; Trachinian landmark pre-eminently famed in antiquity as the site of Herakles' self-immolation and apotheosis.

OMPHALE, Lydian queen to whom Herakles was bound in servitude for a year as atonement for Iphitos' murder.

PALLAS, the goddess Athena, daughter of Zeus and protectress of Herakles, her half-brother.

PARODOS, the entrance song of a tragic chorus.

STASIMON, a danced song composed in pairs of metrically identical stanzas and accompanied by flute; delivered by a tragic chorus between scenes of spoken dialogue; cf. PARODOS.

THEBES, a city in central Greece; birthplace of Herakles.

TIRYNS, a city in southern Greece; Herakles' home during the period of his servitude to Eurystheus.

TRACHIS, a region of central Greece just north of Thermopylai; site of the palace of Keyx and the scene of Herakles' final homecoming.

ZEUS, the supreme Greek deity, "father of gods and men"; actual sire of Herakles.

CPSIA information can be obtained
at www.ICGtesting.com
Printed in the USA
BVHW041053110723
667061BV00015B/67